Prayers
for
Every Day

Nancy Parker Brummett
Lain Ehmann
Marie D. Jones

Publications International, Ltd.

Contributing Writers: Nancy Parker Brummett, Lain Ehmann, and Marie D. Jones

Nancy Parker Brummett is a freelance writer, a columnist, and the author of several books. Leading women closer to the heart of God is the hallmark of her speaking and writing ministries. To learn more about her life and work, visit www.nancyparkerbrummett.com.

Lain Ehmann is a Massachusetts-based writer and the author of *Prayers for Every Month, A Warm Cup of Kindness: Sister,* and many other inspirational books.

Marie D. Jones is the author of *Echoes of Love: Sisters, Mother, Grandmother, Friends, Graduation, Wedding; Mother's Daily Prayer Book;* and *When You Lose Someone You Love: A Year of Comfort.* She can be reached at www.mariedjones.com.

Copyright © 2011 Publications International, Ltd. All rights reserved. This book may not be reproduced or quoted in whole or in part by any means whatsoever without written permission from:

Louis Weber, CEO
Publications International, Ltd.
7373 North Cicero Avenue
Lincolnwood, Illinois 60712

Permission is never granted for commercial purposes.

ISBN-13: 978-1-4508-1452-2
ISBN-10: 1-4508-1452-2

Manufactured in China.

8 7 6 5 4 3 2 1

Library of Congress Control Number: 2010936383

 God Always Listens

*M*any of us reserve our prayers for times when we are in trouble—that is, when we turn to God for strength, for hope, and for help. We do need to pray during those times, but even as we go about the business and "busyness" of our days, we can find the time to turn to God, even if just for a few moments, and ask for his help to overcome the small obstacles and assist us in handling the little challenges. Rather than go to God only in times of great need, we can find the peace, love, and inner calm that comes from communing with him at any time of the day and night.

This special prayer book will help you find the thoughts and feelings you wish to convey to God. They will even inspire you to find your own words, as you turn to God on a daily basis, and ask for what you need. Whether it be his grace, his mercy, or his love when dealing with the relationships in your life or your asking for strength and resilience when life's little detours test your patience, God is right there, waiting to hear from you and give you just what you need to get through the day. No request is too small or too big for God to fulfill, but first we must take the step of becoming quiet and then praying, no matter how crazy our schedules or how tired we are from dealing with family and work. Think about it. God knows what we need even before we do, but we must take that step of asking. And when we ask, God will give us everything we need to live each day to its fullest.

In *Prayers for Every Day,* you can find a way to pray every day and to get into the wonderful habit of continual conversation with a God who would like nothing more than to give you the keys to his kingdom and all that lies within. But first you must ask . . . in prayer. And then, as promised, you shall receive.

January 1

"The Spirit of the Lord is upon me," Jesus proclaimed.
"...to proclaim the year of the Lord's favor."
—Luke 4:18–19

*L*ord, how inadequate for us to set aside one day
in the year on which we are officially thankful. Every
breath we take, every task we undertake, every life
we touch—every part of every day we live should be
offered up to you in gratitude! So, Lord, this coming
year let me truly enter into your gates with praise and
thanksgiving. Your favor is truly upon us because your
Spirit dwells within us. This day is
a beginning of a new year, so
help us begin this year with
joy and celebration for
having been redeemed in
Christ. Amen.

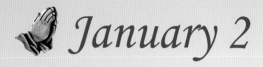# *January 2*

The Father himself loves you.
—John 16:27

*G*od, they say all you need is love, and that is true.
Your loving care has gotten me through so many lumps
and bumps, and you continue to be there for me at
each and every turn on the road of life. My heart
shines with the love that never ceases—the love of you,
my God, who always watches over me and makes clear
my way. You take away my burdens and lighten my
load, and your love smooths the path you have set out
for me. Thank you, God.

*God's love brightens and beautifies
even the darkest days.*

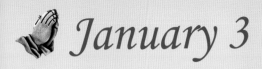 # *January 3*

> *What sort of man is this, that even*
> *the winds and the sea obey him?*
> —Matthew 8:27

*L*ord, even when the storm is raging all around me,
I feel your still, comforting presence. Thank you for
letting me know that no matter how dark the skies
are and regardless of how high the water rises, you are
always with me. You meet me in the midst of the
storm, wherever you find me, and you
calm my troubled spirit. And
so, Lord, I praise you in this
storm. For in it, I find you.

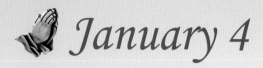# January 4

My grace is sufficient for you.
—2 Corinthians 12:9

Gracious God, of all the gifts you give us, grace may be the most glorious! With your unmerited favor falling upon us, we can survive most anything. Whether in times of plenty or of want, your grace is sufficient. When we feel so exhausted that we don't know how we'll get through the morning, let alone the day, your grace is sufficient. And when serious illness strikes or death is imminent, your grace is sufficient. Thank you, God, for your marvelous and glorious gift of grace.

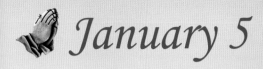 # *January 5*

*Faith is the assurance of things hoped for,
the conviction of things not seen.*
—Hebrews 11:1

$\mathcal{D}$ear Father in heaven, how often our faith seems utterly depleted. We come to you asking for more faith, but we ask for such a small amount. You are willing to douse us with life-giving faith, but we come asking for just what we can carry in our cupped hands. We ask for a bit of faith for a certain situation or the faith to get us through the next task at hand. Please immerse us in a complete renewal of our faith, Lord! Let our faith in you empower us—heart, mind, and soul—that others may see you in all we do.

We never outgrow our need for faith. No one is too strong, too mature, or too experienced to benefit from its grace.

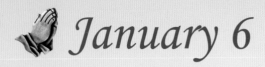 # *January 6*

The Lord will keep you from all evil; he will keep your life.
The Lord will keep your going out and your coming
in from this time on and forevermore.
—Psalm 121:7–8

*H*eavenly Father, there are tough times facing me ahead. I am scared to even wake in the morning, for fear of what the day will bring. Please help me feel your presence and know that I am not alone, though it often feels that way. Please also remind me that no matter what happens on this earth, I have already received the greatest blessing imaginable—salvation through Jesus Christ our Lord. Be with me now and always. Amen.

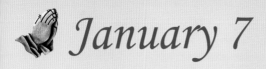 # *January 7*

Who is it that conquers the world but the one who believes
that Jesus is the Son of God?
—1 John 5:5

*Y*es, God, I know what I need to do next. Your words are clear and your meaning is obvious. But why is it so difficult to do what I know I must do? I'm weak in spirit and resolve, for even though I want to do the right thing, I find myself using excuse after excuse not to do it. Please give me the strength and the courage to follow through on my intentions. With your power, I can overcome my hesitations, conquer my fears, and submit to your will for me.

The arms of God are strong enough to guide us
toward a brighter life, free from fear.

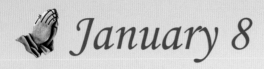 *January 8*

Your word is a lamp to my feet and a light to my path.
—Psalm 119:105

$\mathcal{D}$ear God, this morning I come to you to ask forgiveness for my stubborn insistence on doing everything my own way. Gently and clearly you point out the things I need to let go of, but I hold on to them tenaciously. Forgive me, Lord. Once again, I come to you asking that my will would become less and that your will would become more in me. I want to trust and obey you, for I know that you'll do a much better job with my life than I will. Live in me and through me, Lord. That's my fervent prayer.

Like the lighthouse beacon, faith guides our way through the fog of fear, doubt, and uncertainty to the sea of clarity beyond.

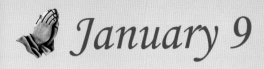 *January 9*

The fruit of the Spirit is love, joy, peace, patience, kindness,
generosity, faithfulness, gentleness, and self-control.
—Galatians 5:22–23

Lord, make me an instrument of thy peace;

where there is hatred, let me sow love;

where there is injury, pardon;

where there is doubt, faith;

where there is despair, hope;

where there is darkness, light;

and where there is sadness, joy.

O Divine Master, grant that I may not so much seek to

be consoled as to console; to be understood, as to

understand; to be loved, as to love; for it is in giving

that we receive, it is in pardoning that we are par-

doned, and it is in dying that we are born to eternal

life. Amen.

—Saint Francis of Assisi

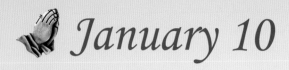 January 10

Blessed be the Lord, for he has heard the sound of my
pleadings. The Lord is my strength and my shield.
—Psalm 28:6–7

God, make me whole again. I have been broken and splintered by the stresses of life and feel as though a huge hole has opened up inside me. It is like a void that only your grace and love can fill. I have tried to fill it with so many things, and I come to you battered by my foolish attempts to find what only you can give me. Renew my body, mind, and spirit, so that I may see things through fresh eyes and face things with new-found energy and willingness. Thanks be to you, God, for making me whole again.

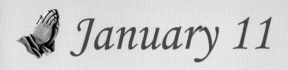 *January 11*

> *Thus says the Lord of hosts: Render true judgments,*
> *show kindness and mercy to one another.*
> —Zechariah 7:9

Where there is suffering, God, let me be an instrument of your loving compassion. Through me, work your miracles to help heal the broken hearts and spirits of those I come in contact with. Let me act as a vessel from which flows caring and hope for those who thirst for it. I want to show others the same compassion you have often shown me and to bring them the good news that they are never alone and never unloved. Thank you, God.

True faith is demonstrated when we look for
ways to be kind to those in need.

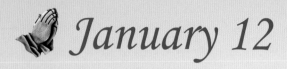# *January 12*

The prayer of the righteous is powerful and effective.

—James 5:16

*F*ather in heaven, you have asked us to pray without ceasing. I am finally beginning to understand what that means. You want us to come to you throughout our day and turn to you first in all situations. We can ask and then hope for our prayers to be granted without fear of reprisal. We can cry to you and express our anger. We can bring you all the cares of our day, and you will receive them for yourself, leaving us free to simply love you. I am awed by your generosity and love, and I thank you over and over again for your steadfastness. Amen.

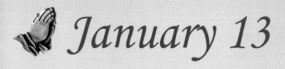# *January 13*

*Out of the believer's heart shall
flow rivers of living water.*
—John 7:38

*H*eavenly Father, light my way today. Make clear to
me where I'm most needed so that I can do your will
and be of service to those less fortunate than I. Guide
me to my highest calling and help me bring out the
best in myself even as I'm constantly tempted with
being less and doing less. When I feel as if I can give
only so much, show me how to give even more so that
the generosity you instill in me may catch on with
others in ever-expanding proportions.

*Seek the goodness that only God
can put in your heart.*

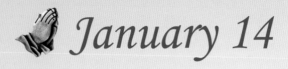# *January 14*

I called on your name, O Lord, from the depths
of the pit; you heard my plea.
—Lamentations 3:55–56

*L*ord, it is so easy to get caught up in my own problems that I forget that there are others far worse off
than I am. Help me find the right perspective by taking
a step back to see that nothing is ever as bad as it
seems. Help me remember that you never give me
more than I am able to handle. Through
your compassion for me, let me be
able to give compassion to those
with far less faith than I have.
Help me, God, to go out to help
others. Amen.

Pray that you will be God's instrument
for bringing good to your world.

# *January 15*

If you forgive others their trespasses, your heavenly Father will also forgive you.
—Matthew 6:14

*F*ather in heaven, thank you so much for the ability to forgive others of their transgressions. It is a blessing to be able to give others the freedom of mercy. And by giving forgiveness to others, I realize what a wonderful gift you have given me in granting me absolution from my sins. Forgiveness is truly divine, and by offering it to others, you allow me to experience godliness in this human body. When I love others, I am closest to our Lord Jesus Christ in deed and spirit.

Love and forgiveness walk hand-in-hand. Our relationships with God and others are intertwined in this dynamic.

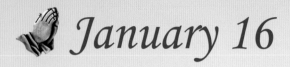# January 16

O Lord my God, I will give thanks to you for ever.
—Psalm 30:12

*L*ord, so many people are blind to the miracles you do in the world around us. They go through life without noticing or experiencing your gifts. They miss the beauty of the natural world, they miss the miracle of love, and they miss the very joy of being alive. Please help me recognize these blessings and also let me help others realize that every second of life is to be cherished and appreciated.

When I first open my eyes upon the morning meadows and look out upon the beautiful world, I thank God I am alive.
—Ralph Waldo Emerson

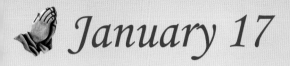# January 17

> *By grace you have been saved.*
> —Ephesians 2:5

*S*upreme Lord, you can't make me new unless I first soften my heart, and yet I'm resistant. Your grace can't take residence within me unless I ask you in, but I've been stubbornly denying you entry. You can't be my salvation until I accept your grace, but I've refused your help. Please, help me offer up every bit of my life to you over and over again until I'm made completely new by the Holy Spirit. I humbly ask in Jesus' wondrous name. Amen.

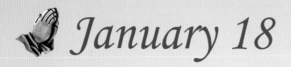# January 18

To all who received him, who believed in his name,
he gave power to become children of God.
—John 1:12

*D*ear heavenly Father, when I was a child, I went
to my mother for comfort. She held me on her lap,
rocked me close to her heart, and wiped away my tears.
When I became an adult, I also became a parent and
had no one to turn to for shelter. That is when I
learned that you are my loving father, my Abba, who
will always hold me close, just as my mother once did.
No matter how old I grow, I can still feel the safety of a
child held in loving arms, comforted and loved beyond
all measure. I know that I am yours, a child of God,
who knows my name and loves me for all eternity.

God's love for us is complete and constant.

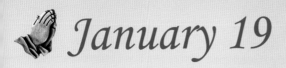 *January 19*

All of us, with unveiled faces, seeing the glory of the Lord as though reflected in a mirror, are being transformed into the same image from one degree of glory to another.
—2 Corinthians 3:18

*L*ord, some days I wonder what's happening to this body of mine. Aches and pains appear for no reason, and the wrinkles are so plentiful there's no use counting anymore. I know you look at inner beauty, not outward beauty, so I come to you to ask you to give me your perspective on this whole aging process. Am I as beautiful in your eyes as I was the day you made me? That's what I choose to believe, Lord, and that's all that really matters to me. Keep making me more beautiful on the inside, and I'll try to make friends with the person in the mirror.

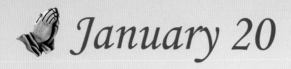# *January 20*

We love because he first loved us.
—1 John 4:19

$\mathcal{L}$ord Jesus, how blessed we are that you left your heavenly kingdom to dwell among us and show us what real love looks like! Without your example, we'd still be looking for love in all the wrong places. Thank you, Lord, for keeping your instruction so simple to understand, even though it's often so hard to follow. Simply love one another, is that it? Okay, Lord, if you say so.

It's the only right response after all you've done for us.

Love God first, and all of your other relationships will fall into place.

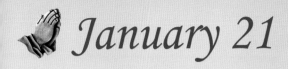 *January 21*

> *You shall see, and your heart shall rejoice; your bodies shall flourish like the grass; and it shall be known that the hand of the Lord is with his servants.*
>
> —Isaiah 66:14

*M*y Lord, I will not lose hope, and I will be a light to others as they struggle in the darkness. I am your faithful servant, and I know that you will never abandon me or leave me in my time of need. I will hold fast to hope as a child holds fast to his mother's hand. I will keep hope alive and spread hope to others wherever I go, knowing that what I give increases the more I give of it. I will not lose hope, Lord, for you are here with me today. Amen.

Offering hope to others through a loving word or a thoughtful act is the surest way to lift your own spirit.

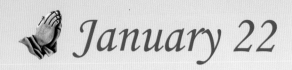 *January 22*

Honor the Lord with your substance and with the first fruits of all your produce; then your barns will be filled with plenty, and your vats will be bursting with wine.
—Proverbs 3:9–10

*B*less me with all good things, heavenly Father, and show me how to share those blessings with others. Open the kingdom of heaven to me, and let me walk in its beauty and bounty with those I love. Set straight the path before me, and let me take the road you have planned for me, the road to abundant joy and prosperity. Bless me in such a way that I will feel compelled to share your blessings with others.

Speaking God's Word in love blesses others.

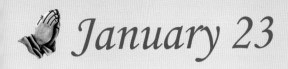

January 23

The steadfast love of the Lord never ceases, his mercies never come to an end; they are new every morning; great is your faithfulness.

—Lamentations 3:22–23

*D*ear Lord God, when we look at your faithfulness, we truly stand in awe. No matter how seriously we take the promises we make or how dedicated we are to those we love, our faithfulness can never compare to yours. You, O Lord, are truly faithful! You are faithful to forgive. You are faithful to fulfill all your promises to your people. Thank you, Lord, for your faithfulness to all generations, now and forever. Amen.

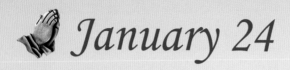# January 24

*The Peace of God, which surpasses all understanding, will
guard your hearts and your minds in Christ Jesus.*

—Philippians 4:7

*L*ord, we stand on your promises, but when it comes
to your promise that your peace is with us, we sometimes stand confused. Where is your peace when young
soldiers are killed in war? Where is your peace in
the middle of the night when a sick child cannot be
comforted? Where is your peace when a marriage is
irretrievably broken? Yet even when we cannot see
your peace, Lord, we know it is there because of your
promise. We can find it in these and all circumstances
when we come to you humbly and ask you for it.
Thank you for your unfailing promise of peace.

*True help and real peace are to be found from
trusting in God's guidance and inspiration.*

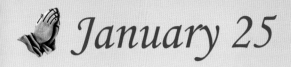

January 25

> *Ask, and it will be given you; search, and you will find;*
> *knock, and the door will be opened for you. For everyone*
> *who asks receives, and everyone who searches finds, and*
> *for everyone who knocks, the door will be opened.*
> —Matthew 7:7–8

*F*ather in heaven, you tell us that whatever we ask for, you will give us. Lately, though, I feel as though you haven't heard my prayers. I believe you are faithful and loving, wanting only the best for me. So I come to you in prayer to ask again, and to thank you, for I am certain in time you will answer my prayers in ways I cannot even imagine. Thank you for being a loving God, allowing me to petition you for all my heart's desires. Amen.

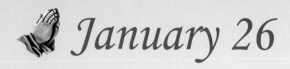 # *January 26*

*When you reap your harvest in your field and forget a sheaf
in the field, you shall not go back to get it; it shall be left for
the alien, the orphan, and the widow, so that the Lord
your God may bless you in all your undertakings.*
—Deuteronomy 24:19

*D*ear Lord, you have blessed me so much today that
I ask that you give some of that wonderful merciful
generosity of yours to someone who needs it more.
I have so much, and my heart bursts in gratitude, but
nothing would make me happier than to see others
blessed just as I have been. And if there is a way for me
to be a blessing to someone, please send them my way.
Sometimes the best gift I can give is the gift of myself,
so let me give myself to someone in need today.

A joy that is shared is a joy made double.
—English Proverb

# *January 27*

Blessed be the God and Father of our Lord Jesus Christ! By his great mercy he has given us a new birth into a living hope through the resurrection of Jesus Christ from the dead.
—1 Peter 1:3

*A*lmighty Father, so many people in this world feel completely hopeless. The jobless feel hopeless. The homeless feel hopeless. The unpopular teenager feels hopeless. The overwhelmed mother feels hopeless. Today, loving Father, present yourself to them so they can readily see the source of all hope. Shine a light on each situation, dear Father—a light that casts out the darkness of hopelessness. For there is no such thing as hopelessness in your presence.

Choosing to live as people of hope is to cling to God's promise that he will make all things new.

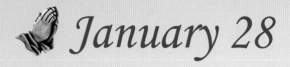

January 28

Now my head is lifted up above my enemies all around me,
and I will offer in his tent sacrifices with shouts of joy;
I will sing and make melody to the Lord.
—Psalm 27:6

*H*oly God, be with me today. I am entering a battle-
field, and I am girding myself with your armor. I have
a war against evil to fight, and though the enemy is
strong, I know that righteousness will prevail. I go
forth in complete peace knowing that you are in
control, that I am in your care, and that
I have nothing to fear. I need no
other protection than you, for you
are with me today, tomorrow, and
always. Amen.

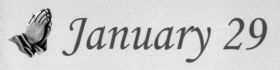

January 29

I have loved you with an everlasting love;
therefore I have continued my faithfulness to you.
—Jeremiah 31:3

When other people let me down, Father in heaven, it is good to know that I can always count on you to get me by. Sometimes my friends and family are too busy or distracted to deal with my simple needs, so in prayer I come to you asking for your understanding and for an increased faith in your devotion to me. There are too few people and things in life we can depend on, but I believe you will always be there for me when I need it. Thank you, loving Father, for giving me something truly wonderful to believe in.

Faith in God's love frees me, for I remember
that God sees me as I am and
loves me with all his heart.

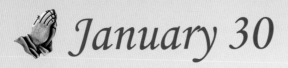 *January 30*

How you have helped one who has no power!
How you have assisted the arm that has no strength!
How you have counseled one who has no wisdom,
and given much good advice!
—Job 26:2–3

*E*veryone thinks they know what is best for me, my Lord, but I turn to you for the wisdom I seek to live the best life I can. For you alone know my purpose and my destiny, and you alone know the best way for me to fulfill your plan for me in this life. Although I consider the counsel of others, it is your Word and will that I'll obey. I pray that I'll always surrender to your divine direction, letting it guide me to a place of perfect love and peace. May I always follow where you lead me, Lord Jesus.

We make our own plans, but it is God who leads the way and clears the obstacles from our path.

# January 31

> *God proves his love for us in that while we still*
> *were sinners Christ died for us.*
> —Romans 5:8

*D*ear heavenly Father, every time I think of your sacrifice for us, I am overwhelmed. That you would give so much for us is almost inconceivable. There are no possible words to express the depth of love you have for us and no possible way to repay it. So I will simply say, "Thank you." Thank you for being our Father in heaven, and thank you for giving us the opportunity to love you in return. In the name of your precious Son, Jesus Christ, I pray. Amen.

My Prayer Life

_____

_____

_____

_____

_____

_____

_____

_____

_____

_____

_____

_____

_____

_____

_____

_____

_____

_____

_____

February 1

Do not judge, and you will not be judged;
do not condemn, and you will not be condemned.
Forgive, and you will be forgiven.
—Luke 6:37

Lord, before I can feel compassion, I must let go
of my need to assign blame when problems occur
or mistakes happen. Assigning blame is just another
way of judging, and you have told us repeatedly that
judgment comes at your hands, not ours. I ask that you
help me to move past the need to blame others and
instead work on acceptance and love. If I can accept
the situation without needing to blame someone for
its creation, we can all work together to find a solution
rather than focusing on who is at fault. And when we
all work together in your name, miracles can occur. In
this I ask your blessing. Amen.

Truly, forgiveness is a healing gift from above.

 # February 2

I lift up my eyes to the hills—from where will my help come?
My help comes from the Lord, who made heaven and earth.

—Psalm 121:1–2

$\mathcal{L}$ord, I was just with my friend. You know the incredible hurt she is feeling right now. Please give me your wisdom and insight so that I can figure out how to lighten her burden—even if just a little. Show me, Lord, what I can say or do to help her through this hard time. And during this struggle, may we grow closer in our friendship as we each also grow closer to you.

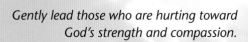

Gently lead those who are hurting toward
God's strength and compassion.

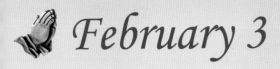# *February 3*

Beloved, let us love one another, because love is from God;
everyone who loves is born of God and knows God.

—1 John 4:7

*J*esus, one of my relationships is faltering, and we
need your presence. I have faith that you can make all
things new again, and you can revive even those things
that seem to be beyond hope. I ask that you help us
shed our old ways of acting and reacting, that we may
make a new relationship, dedicated to and consecrated
in you. With your help, we can heal past hurts and
forge new ways of relating that will bring us closer to
you, together and individually. Please be with us as we
work on this challenge. Amen.

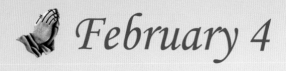

February 4

The Lord is gracious and merciful, slow to anger
and abounding in steadfast love.

—Psalm 145:8

*I*t has been said that resentment is like taking poison and expecting someone else to die. God, please free me from the chains of past resentment that I might find a lightness of being when I let go of the bonds of the hurt and injustice done to me. I want to have peace in my heart and in my life, and I know I won't until I find a way to accept the past, to forgive those who have wronged me, and to move on with my life. Help me break those chains and bonds, God, and free my spirit to soar.

Even if we feel we've been wronged by someone, we should soften our hearts and forgive the one who wronged us. Then the burden of bitterness will be lifted.

# February 5

*Grace to you and peace from God our Father
and the Lord Jesus Christ.*
—Philemon 3

Lord in heaven, your grace is given to me as my birthright in Jesus Christ. Nevertheless, I find myself hardening my heart against others, thinking that they do not "deserve" my kindness or my time. What a hypocrite I am! Nothing I have ever done has made me worthy of your sacrifice to me—the one who is ever willing to judge others. Please forgive me for my pride, and help me open myself to all my Christian brothers and sisters. I ask in the holy name of Jesus Christ. Amen.

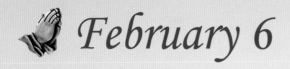 # February 6

The Lord gives wisdom; from his mouth come knowledge and understanding.

—Proverbs 2:6

God, I admit that there are many times in my day that I forget to focus on what I have. I am so consumed with what I want and need that I often lose track of the amazing and abundant blessings you have already given me. Please help me shift my focus back to the good things that surround me, no matter how simple they might be. Too often I find myself worrying about my life, wanting to do more and achieve more and have more, and then I am without peace. Guide me back to that place within where I am aware of all the treasures you have placed before me.

May you know that a wisdom and a love transcend the things you will see and touch today.

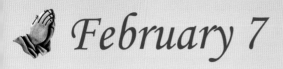# *February 7*

God did not give us a spirit of cowardice, but rather a spirit of power and of love and of self-discipline.
—2 Timothy 1:7

*S*upreme Lord of the universe, today I stand strong and proclaim your glory. My faith in you makes me strong, and I can't help but share my trust and love for you with others. You are the sovereign Lord, and all that you declare shall come to pass. Nothing can withstand your will, and I'm thankful to align myself with you. I'm in awe of your power and glory, and my heart is full of your Holy Spirit. When I read your Word, I'm reassured of your promises to me. I want nothing more than to live as a follower of Christ until the end of my days.

God gives us faith as a means of getting in touch with his love.

February 8

Now may our Lord Jesus Christ himself and God our Father,
who loved us and through grace gave us eternal comfort
and good hope, comfort your hearts.
—2 Thessalonians 2:16–17

*M*y Lord, I come across so many people with misguided hopes. Their hopes are in their ability to make a lot of money, their athletic skills, or their academic acumen. Maybe their hopes are in their husbands, their wives, or even in their children through which they vicariously pursue their own lost dreams. As they move from one disappointment to the next, Lord, reach out to show them that the only sure place for them to put their hope is in you. Thank you, Lord.

God will either give you what you ask,
or something far better.
—Robert Murray McCheyne

February 9

The human mind plans the way,
but the Lord directs the steps.
—Proverbs 16:9

*D*ear Lord, all my plans have been tossed in the air like so many grains of rice, never to be gathered or ordered again. I thought I had it all figured out, but now I find that I'm powerless. You remind me once again that I'm not in control and that the only sure thing is you. I'm scared, but I know that I can regain my footing. Please help me find the right path—not the path of my choosing but the path you have planned for me.

Turn over your problems to God, and he will
orchestrate the best outcome.

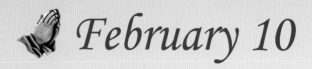

February 10

No one has greater love than this,
to lay down one's life for one's friends.
—John 15:13

God, they say you get by with a little help from your friends, and I know that to be true. Thank you for filling my life and my days with good friends who care about me. Each one is like an angel sent down from heaven in human form, and I cherish them all. So today I ask that you keep my friendships strong and true, no matter how much time or distance may separate us as we all live our lives. Keep them close where it counts—in my heart. Thank you.

A true friend is the greatest of all blessings.
—Duc de la Rochefoucauld

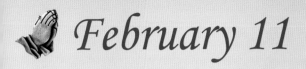

February 11

Therefore love truth and peace.
—Zechariah 8:19

*L*ord, we often think of peace as something that comes when we're ready, when our hands are folded and our minds quiet. But your love and presence are in all things of this world, the loud and the quiet, the raging river as well as the silent pond. You are everywhere, and it is as likely to hear you on a bustling city street as it is in the isolated silence of a redwood forest. Please remind me that I can find your peace anywhere if my eyes are open and my heart is willing. Amen.

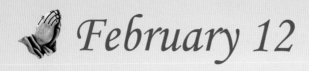

February 12

The Lord bless you and keep you; the Lord make his face to shine upon you, and be gracious to you; the Lord lift up his countenance upon you, and give you peace.

—Numbers 6:24–26

*A*lmighty God, help me open my heart to all the blessings you have offered me. I go through life numb, blind, and deaf, unable to sense what you have placed in front of me. Please help me raise my eyes from the ground and instead focus them on the world around me, taking in all of your creations and appreciating them for what they are—testaments of your love for me and all humankind.

God's divine essence is evident in the eyes of a believer.

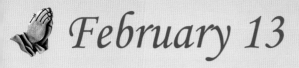

February 13

[Jesus] said to the woman,
"Your faith has saved you; go in peace."
—Luke 7:50

Lord, bring peace to my heart and rest to my soul.
These trying times leave me anxious and worried for
my future and for those I love. I am struggling to find
a sense of inner calm and ask for the peace that passes
all understanding, the peace your love
and grace can bring. I ask this not just
for me but also for all those who
long for calm in the storms of
life. Peace be to us all. Amen.

February 14

*For we are the aroma of Christ to God
among those who are being saved.*
—2 Corinthians 2:15

*T*he love you give me, God, can carry me through my
life. I have no need for anything else, for with your
love comes the kingdom and all that it offers. Your love
is like the most priceless riches, a treasure trove that
never ends. It always provides me with everything I
need to be happy, healthy, and free. I depend on your
love, and I share that love with those I come in contact
with, knowing that as I give, I shall receive more. Your
love is my treasure, God. Thank you. Amen.

What we love we shall grow to resemble.
—St. Bernard of Clairvaux

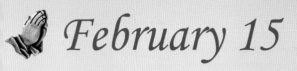 *February 15*

Be kind to one another, tenderhearted, forgiving one another,
as God in Christ has forgiven you.
—Ephesians 4:32

Teach me, my Lord, to be kind and gentle in all the events of life; in disappointments, in the thoughtlessness of others, in the insincerity of those I trusted, and in the unfaithfulness of those on whom I relied. Let me put myself aside to think of the happiness of others, and to hide my little pains and heartaches so that I may be the only one to suffer from them. Teach me to profit by the suffering that comes across my path. Let me so use it that it may mellow me, not harden nor embitter me; that it may make me patient, not irritable; and that it may make me broad in my forgiveness, not narrow, haughty or overbearing.

Growing in wisdom means growing in love,
tolerance, grace, and acceptance.
—"Following Christ," *The Pilgrim's Prayer Book*

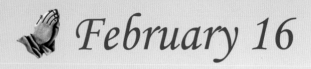

February 16

So even to old age and gray hairs, O God, do not forsake me,
until I proclaim your might to all the generations to come.
—Psalm 71:18

*F*ather God, when will we learn that the greatest gift we can pass to our children and our grandchildren is not our earthly wealth but our faith in you? We set up trust funds and college funds, or we feel badly when we can't, when the only true security is through you. As parents and grandparents, keep us focused on what really matters. Remind us to spend precious time with the younger generation—to earn the right to share the greatest legacy we have to give, which is faith in you.

Go forth in the joy of the Lord, knowing
how blessed you are.

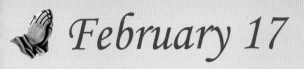

February 17

Let your light shine before others, so that they may see your
good works and give glory to your Father in heaven.

—Matthew 5:16

*H*eavenly Lord, I long to be a blessing to those
around me and to share the love for you I have gained
through studying your holy Word. Today, please help
me sense the needs of those around me. Let me offer
a word of encouragement, extend a hand in help, or
stop for a moment to listen to someone who
just needs to talk. Let your light shine
through me so that others may find
their way to Christ.

February 18

*The Lord your God . . . executes justice for the orphan
and the widow, and . . . loves the strangers,
providing them food and clothing.*

—Deuteronomy 10:17–18

*L*ord, I pray that my words and actions may be a
comfort to those in need. Let me see the world around
me through your eyes, that I might notice the small
wounds and sorrows that each of us carries within,
hidden from view and known only to you. I ask that
you use my hands to do your work here on earth, to
heal the hurting, to feed the hungry, and to reach out
to the lonely. May I be an instrument of your endless
love that I might share your
spirit generously and abundantly
with everyone I encounter.

 # *February 19*

Be strong, and let your heart take courage,
all you who wait for the Lord.
—Psalm 31:24

Lord in heaven, many days I feel like your servant David, who at times was persecuted and hated and who at times was alone except for your presence. While I do not know why you have given me these burdens to carry, I do know that with your help I can bear them. Each day, I awake with my heart filled with hope that a better life awaits me, if not here on earth, then someday in your heavenly presence.

Our trust and faithfulness produce the endurance that sees us through the trials we all face in this life.

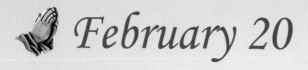 *February 20*

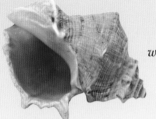

Do not say, "I will repay evil";
wait for the Lord, and he will help you.
—Proverbs 20:22

*H*eavenly Father, there is so much hatred in this
world. It's on the front page of every newspaper and
the lead story of the nightly news. We all are obsessed
about getting what's due to us and about punishing
those who have taken what we think belongs to us, but
the only way to peace is through forgiveness. Please
teach us that hurting each other is not the solution.
Instead, help us all feel your mercy and pass it on to
those we encounter each day. Amen.

We need to be understanding and practice
forgiveness in our daily lives.

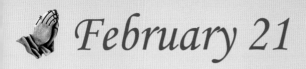

February 21

*I am reminded of your sincere faith, a faith that lived first
in your grandmother... and your mother.*
—2 Timothy 1:5

*T*oday, Lord, I want to lift up all the mothers of
young children to you. Their days can seem so long,
Lord, and the expressions of appreciation for what
they do can be so few and far between. Please renew
them with the understanding that they are doing
mighty and meaningful work. Smile down on them
today, Lord, wherever they may be, and give them the
encouragement and the confidence that only comes
from you. Assure them that you see every shoe they tie,
every spill they clean up, and every little tear they dry.
Each time they hug their children, may they feel your
arms around them. Thank you, Lord.

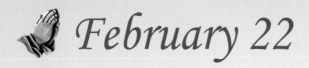

February 22

Blessings are on the head of the righteous.
—Proverbs 10:6

*H*eavenly Father, I thank you for the abundance of blessings you continue to bring into my life. I appreciate my family and friends, the walls around me, the clothing I wear, and the food I eat. Each and every one of these comes only through your love and continued devotion to me. All that I am, all that I have, all that I will be is because of you. Amen.

All our opportunities, abilities, and resources come from God to hold in sacred trust for him.

February 23

Teach me to do your will, for you are my God.
Let your good spirit lead me on a level path.
—Psalm 143:10

*O*God, all the instruction and guidance we need to
live a purposeful life is provided for us in your Word.
So why do we find ourselves allured by commentators
on talk shows or by self-help gurus with all the latest
and purportedly greatest approaches to life's problems? Keep me in your perfect will for my life, Lord,
and prevent me from being pulled
this way and that by all the influences
this world promotes. For I know that
it is only when you are leading me
that I'm moving in the right
direction.

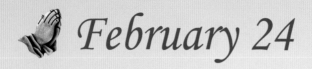

February 24

For by grace you have been saved through faith, and this is not your own doing; it is the gift of God—not the result of works, so that no one may boast.

—Ephesians 2:8–9

*A*mazing grace! That's certainly what grace is, Father in heaven—truly amazing! Grace that gives a sinner entrance into heaven. Grace that reaches down to heal the sick and lift up the poorest of the poor. Grace that changes hearts in an instant. Grace that saved a wretch like me. O Lord, how we thank you for the gift of grace. By your mercy you created a wonderful path to salvation—one that's open to everyone because it's not about what we do but about what you did. Thank you, Father. We praise you for your amazing grace!

It is God and God alone who gives me power to walk through dark valleys into the light again.

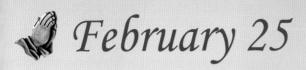

February 25

Sing praises to the Lord, for he has done gloriously; let this be known in all the earth. Shout aloud and sing for joy.
—Isaiah 12:5–6

*T*hank you for going with me on my walk today, Lord. You know how exhausted I was when I started out. But the longer I walked, the more things I thought about to bring to you in prayer, the more aware I became of your awesome creation all around me, and the more rejuvenated I became. Sending those three deer by my path was an especially nice touch. You are the bounce in my step, Lord. Thanks for the walk.

God writes the gospel not in the Bible alone,
but on trees, and flowers, and clouds and stars.
—Martin Luther

February 26

The Lord is king! Let the earth rejoice.
—Psalm 97:1

*A*lmighty God, how creative you are! Within the elements of your creation are hidden messages of wonder, encouragement, and love. A purple hyacinth breaks through the snow by a rural mailbox, and the message of hope is delivered. A single cardinal swoops down and flies beside the car of someone who is grieving as if to say, "Be assured! God sees your grief and is with you." A tiny kitten seems to seek the saddest person in the room and curls up in her lap. Thank you, Lord, for touching us through your creation. How very blessed we are!

February 27

Bear with one another and, if anyone has a complaint against another, forgive each other; just as the Lord has forgiven you, so you also must forgive.
—Colossians 3:13

I am not sure, heavenly Father, that I can ever forget this pain. I know that time will heal all wounds, and that one day I will look back on this as a lesson learned and wisdom gained. But right now, I struggle to keep from letting anger and depression overcome me. Help me find that middle road, where I can forgive, even if I am not yet able to forget. I long to be free of the dark fog that envelops me, and I pray that you will embolden me to step forward and move beyond what was done to me to the hope of what will be.

God's healing balm grants the freedom that forgiveness brings.

February 28

*My friends, if anyone is detected in a transgression,
you who have received the Spirit should restore
such a one in a spirit of gentleness.*
—Galatians 6:1

*H*eavenly Father, I long to have your wisdom. I want
to model myself on you, never reacting out of haste or
anger, but pausing to reflect before answering another's
behaviors or words. I want to take a moment to put
myself in their place, taking on their hurts and sorrows, so I may respond from a place of kindness and
compassion rather than thoughtlessness or impatience.
Help me become more like you in this
way so that others may feel loved
and understood by me. Amen.

*Let the beams of God's goodness
shine through you.*

February 29

> [Jesus said,] "Love your enemies and pray for those who
> persecute you, so that you may be children of your Father in
> heaven; for he makes his sun rise on the evil and on the good,
> and sends rain on the righteous and on the unrighteous."
>
> —Matthew 5:44–45

Our Creator, sometimes it's hard for us to understand why people who don't live a life of faith seem tremendously blessed. But what they don't know, and we should, is that they are the beneficiaries of your common grace—the grace you bestow on all those you created. Forgive us for being resentful or envious, Lord. Nothing on this earth compares to the riches of salvation that are ours. Therefore, we pray for those who don't know the source of their blessing. Introduce them to your grace, now and forever.

*Mercy, grace, and love are always available
to us, for the Lord is always available to us.*

My Prayer Life

_____

_____

_____

_____

_____

_____

_____

_____

_____

_____

_____

_____

_____

_____

_____

_____

_____

_____

_____

_____

March 1

My brothers and sisters, whenever you face trials of any kind, consider it nothing but joy.
—James 1:2

*L*ord, it seems strange to be thanking you for the pain I've experienced in my life. But from the perspective of time, I can see that each of these challenges has helped me become a more loving and compassionate person. If I had never felt disappointment, I would not have helped those who have failed as I have. If I had never felt heartbreak, I would not have helped those whose hearts are empty as mine was. If I had never been the target of hatred, I would not have suffered with those who are hated as I was. My own suffering has opened me to the suffering of others, and it makes me long to help them heal. And for this, I thank you.

Our own self-worth is developed as we help and serve others.

 # *March 2*

Then your light shall break forth like the dawn, and your healing shall spring up quickly; your vindicator shall go before you, the glory of the Lord shall be your rear guard.
—Isaiah 58:8

I have faith in you, Lord Jesus, for you have never let me down. My faith makes me strong and fills me with the courage and fortitude I need to get through life's more pressing problems. Your faith in me is like a beacon that I move toward, helping my eyes focus on the prize of your love and on your assistance in all that I do. Knowing that I'm not alone helps me be a pillar of strength for others as well, as they discover their own lost faith in you. I have faith in you, Lord. You always come through for me. Thank you.

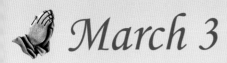

March 3

O give thanks to the Lord, call on his name, make known his
deeds among the peoples. Sing to him, sing praises
to him, tell of all his wonderful works.
—1 Chronicles 16:8–9

*H*eavenly Father, accept my thanksgiving for the wonderful life you have given me. My family is healthy, my work is fulfilling, and I feel a deep sense of peace that I have not felt for a long time. I am truly grateful to you for continuously proving to me that your will is always better than mine and that your point of view is much bigger and broader than the narrow perceptions of my little life. In gratitude I live each day knowing that there is peace in my life when I look beyond the surface of things to where you are: always present, always there. Amen.

Give thanks and praise for what you have, and
your prayers are already answered.

March 4

A new heart I will give you, and a new spirit I will put within you; and I will remove from your body the heart of stone and give you a heart of flesh.

—Ezekiel 36:26

*L*ord, because you know me well, you know that there was a time in my life when I was so busy and moving so fast that I didn't notice the birds. How sad is that? I am truly grateful to you for slowing me down, Lord. Now when I see birds at my feeder, along with all the other wonders of your miraculous creation, my heart overflows with thanksgiving. I wouldn't have wanted to miss this glorious world of yours, Lord. Thank you for getting my attention.

Our Creator's hand is always at work making us better than we know we can be.

 *March 5*

Let the word of Christ dwell in you richly.
—Colossians 3:16

$\mathcal{H}$eavenly Father, when you came to earth to show us how to live, you did so not for your own glory, but out of love for us. In turn, your rules are ways that you show your love, not an attempt to control or thwart our free will. By giving us guidelines, you are helping us live fulfilling, spiritual, and safe lives. When I follow your commandments, it is a way of showing you how much I love you in return. Please help me remember how to love you every day. Amen.

When we let Christ become the source of our wisdom, he will guide us in making wise decisions and acting on them.

 # *March 6*

> *If my people who are called by my name humble themselves,*
> *pray, seek my face, and turn from their wicked ways,*
> *then I will hear from heaven, and will forgive*
> *their sin and heal their land.*
>
> —2 Chronicles 7:14

*O*God, how we have wreaked havoc in this land you created for us! Lord, we are guilty of calling evil good and good evil. We have erected false idols before you in the form of wealth, success, beauty, or athletic achievement, and to these false idols we give far too much attention and allegiance. All around us we see the consequences of greed and self-destruction. We claim we are too busy to pray and too overbooked to worship. Lord, we humbly come to you now and ask you to forgive us. And please, Lord, heal our land.

God will eagerly forgive our mistakes in the
hope that we will learn and grow from them.

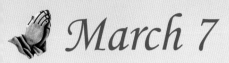

March 7

We urge you, beloved, to admonish the idlers, encourage the faithhearted, help the weak, be patient with all of them.
—1 Thessalonians 5:14

God, let me be a comfort to someone who needs me today. As you have always comforted me in rough times, let me do the same for someone who is sad, ill, or suffering and needs to know they are cared for. Guide me toward those I can be of loving service to, and let no opportunity pass me to do something good in the world today. If someone is in need, send him my way. If someone is depressed, have her call me. Let me be a comfort to those who feel they cannot go on alone. I am at your service today, God. Make use of me. Amen.

# *March 8*

*Hope does not disappoint us, because God's love has been
poured into our hearts through the Holy Spirit
that has been given to us.*

—Romans 5:5

One day at a time, heavenly Father. I think I can find
the hope within to take this crazy world one day at
a time. When the stresses of life overwhelm me, you
remind me that you are willing to carry my burdens.
You will take the weight of the yoke that is upon my
neck and free me from all anxiety. One day at a time—
hope is the thing I hold on to as I accept what is and
look to what will be when this, too, shall pass. One
day at a time, dear Father, with hope in my heart, I
continue on.

Hope is faith holding out its hand in the dark.

— George Iles

 *March 9*

*The Lord watch between you and me,
when we are absent one from the other.*
—Genesis 31:49

*H*eavenly Father, how blessed we are! You keep us connected to those we love even when they are far away. When a mom in one city prays while her college-age daughter is praying in another city, they are connected by their prayers to you. I want to be connected that way to my family far away, Lord. You know how much I miss them all. Comfort my yearning heart and empty arms with the knowledge that we are never really separated from those we love, especially when we all love you. Thank you for that blessing, Lord.

# March 10

Now, our God, we give thanks to you
and praise your glorious name.
—1 Chronicles 29:13

Dear God, for another day, for another minute, for

another chance to live and serve you, I am grateful.

Please...fill me...

With love that knows no bounds,

With sympathy that reaches all,

With courage that cannot be shaken,

With faith strong enough for the darkness,

With strength sufficient for my tasks,

With loyalty to your kingdom,

With wisdom to meet life's mysteries,

With power to lift me to yourself.

Be with me for another day and

use me as you will. Amen.

—"The Daily Offering," from *The Pilgrim's Prayer Book*

March 11

Let every person be subject to the governing authorities; for there is no authority except from God, and those authorities that exist have been instituted by God.

—Romans 13:1

*D*ear Lord, we come to you today, and we humbly beseech you to continue guiding our country in the direction you want it to go. Many things about our country and our culture are changing, Lord, and we need your help in understanding which changes are for good and which are taking us places you never intended for us to go. Guide the leaders of our country, Lord—those in elected positions and those in other positions of influence. And finally, dear Lord, guide our thoughts, our words, and our actions that we may be good stewards of this marvelous country you've given us. We ask that you never lift your hand of protection from us. It is in your all-powerful name that we pray to you. Amen.

# *March 12*

*Lord, . . . grant to your servants to speak your word with
all boldness, while you stretch out your hand to heal,
and signs and wonders are performed through
the name of your holy servant Jesus.*

—Acts 4:29–30

*L*ord Jesus Christ, in you and through you all things
are possible. As your dedicated servant, I ask that you
allow me to do great things in your name. There is too
much want and strife in this world, and I'm insignifi-
cant and powerless without you. I am here, with hands
open and outstretched, hoping that you will enable me
to spread your grace to others. It would be my greatest
joy to be able to relieve the pain of others on your
behalf. Please use me to do your will.

*Compassion clothes the heart
of every faithful Christian.*

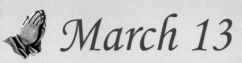# March 13

This is my commandment, that you love one
another as I have loved you.
—John 15:12

*H*oly God, may your peace visit our household. May
you be with us when we rise, helping us set our schedules for the day. May you be with us each minute as we
go through our routines. May you be with us as we sit
down to eat together, and may you be with us as we
lay down to sleep at night. May each member of our
family acknowledge your presence, feel your loving
hand, and rest in your peace. Amen.

Peace in the family is the consciousness that
there is an unfailing wealth of love and
devotion and fidelity to fall back upon.
— Harry Emerson Fosdick

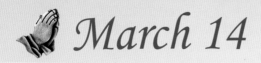# *March 14*

*You, O Lord, are a God merciful and gracious, slow to anger
and abounding in steadfast love and faithfulness.*
—Psalm 86:15

God, today I pray not for myself but for my friends
and my family. I ask that you shine your loving light
upon them for all the good they do. Bless them with all
good things. Without my friends and family, I don't
know how I would get by. I know in my heart that you
sent each and every one of them to
me; they were handpicked by you
with love. Bless my friends today.

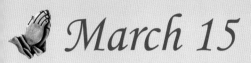

March 15

Wisdom is a fountain of life to one who has it.
—Proverbs 16:22

$\mathcal{B}$e with all our teachers, loving Father. Our children are so blessed by the sacrifices that these teachers make each day as they pass along their academic wisdom, as well as their common sense. Give them an abundance of both, Lord. And please keep the schools in which they work safe from harm. Today, may teachers feel inspired and gratified, and may the appreciation they so richly deserve be showered upon them. Lord, as the greatest teacher of all, instill your insights in all those who endeavor to teach today.

*It is a teacher's servant heart
that can keep her or him going.*

# March 16

Direct your heart to the Lord, and serve him only, and he will deliver you.

—1 Samuel 7:3

*F*ather, it is not easy to remain hopeful in the face of adversity. Sometimes I just want to run away from the challenges I face or hide in my bed and cry. But because you have told us to be joyful in our hope, I will put away my fears and replace them with steadfast trust in you. I'm confident that you will deliver me, and I will use this time to grow in my belief in you. I ask in the name of your precious Son. Amen.

# *March 17*

> *For God alone my soul waits in silence; from him comes my salvation. He alone is my rock and my salvation, my fortress; I shall never be shaken.*
>
> —Psalm 62:1–2

*H*eavenly God, I come to you in prayer and thanksgiving. I praise you for your love and mercy, for each of the blessings you have given me throughout my days. You know my needs before I even know them myself, and you fulfill my heart's desires. You comfort me in times of trouble, hold me in times of sadness, and rejoice with me in times of happiness. You are, indeed, my rock and my salvation. Praise be your name!

Today, may I feel grateful for those moments when something heavenly graces my daily routine.

# March 18

He will command his angels concerning you, to protect you.
—Luke 4:10

$\mathcal{D}$ear God, even though I feel alone, I know you are with me. Every step I take is guided by your loving hand, and you will never leave me. I can't see the road ahead, but you can, for you know all the dangers and obstacles. If I put my trust in you, you will keep me safe, protecting me from my enemies and from my own weaknesses. Please be with me, now and forever.

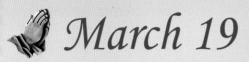 *March 19*

When the ways of people please the Lord, he causes even
their enemies to be at peace with them.
—Proverbs 16:7

*G*od, it is so easy to feel empathy and compassion for
those I love and care about. But what about the people
in my life who hurt me and who drive me up the wall?
I feel so angry and short with them, yet I know that you
would want me to treat them the same way I would ask
to be treated. It is hard to be kind to those who are
unkind, but I know it is your will, dear God. So today
I pray for character and virtue, so I can show the same
compassion to my enemies that I do my friends.

Forgiveness is the central virtue in God's
treasure chest—God's forgiveness of us and
our forgiveness of others and ourselves.

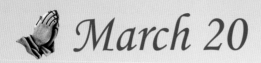# *March 20*

*Now that faith has come, we are no longer subject to
a disciplinarian, for in Christ Jesus you are
all children of God through faith.*

—Galatians 3:25–26

*T*o those who have faith, more good things shall be
given. Faith in you, God, multiplies blessings and
makes the old shine like new again. To those who have
faith, nothing is impossible under the sun, and all
things can be overcome. To those who have faith, love
and hope are never far from sight, even when it seems
they have abandoned us. To those who have faith in
you, God, the kingdom is set out before us to live
amidst the infinite abundance and unlimited prosperity of your promises. Thanks be to you, the one, true
God. Amen.

*We should always thank the Lord
for the faith of others.*

March 21

Truly I tell you, this poor widow has put in more than all those who are contributing to the treasury. For all of them have contributed out of their abundance; but she out of her poverty has put in everything she had, all she had to live on.
—Mark 12:43–44

God, how can I ever thank you enough for the blessings in my life? Each time I turn around, I see something to be grateful for, some small miracle that makes my heart sing and reminds me that you are always present and always working for my highest good. I thank you for the daily joys that greet me when I rise each morning and for the calm and peace that is in my heart knowing that I am always being loved, watched over, and cared for. Thank you, God.

When you open your eyes to the bountiful blessings already in your life, you realize just how abundant the world really is.

March 22

*All the trees of the field shall know that I am the Lord. I bring
low the high tree, I make high the low tree. I dry up
the green tree and make the dry tree flourish.*
—Ezekiel 17:24

*F*ather in heaven, you are the Creator of all that lives
in this world, including all the trees in the fields. You
have the power to give life and to take life. And so, I
want to sing a new song so all can hear me. I want my
lips to praise your name and also to proclaim the
rebirth of hope in Jesus Christ. I long to be a beacon
for others and show them the path to new life through
you. I offer myself to you to be used for your purposes.
Find my sacrifice pleasing in your sight. It is not much,
but it is all I have to offer. I ask this in the name of
your Son, Jesus Christ. Amen.

*God's grace can refresh and renew us with
the living water of hope and faith.*

# March 23

Know that wisdom is such to your soul; if you find it, you will find a future, and your hope will not be cut off.

—Proverbs 24:14

*H*eavenly Father, today I need to ask you to forgive me for frittering away my time. Time is such a precious gift, and I know that so well. But instead of using time wisely today, I wasted too much of it mindlessly watching television. Even sitting alone and possibly praying would be a better use of my time, Father. Forgive me for wasting one of your most precious gifts to me. And thank you that tomorrow is another day and another opportunity to spend my time wisely.

March 24

Pray in the Spirit at all times in every prayer and
supplication. To that end keep alert and always
persevere in supplication for all the saints.
—Ephesians 6:18

Dear God, I deserve nothing more from you, for you have already given me the greatest gift I could ever hope for—that is, your only begotten Son, Jesus Christ. But you have told me to come to you for all things, and so I have even more to ask. You know what my heart longs for, and even more, you know what I need. In your grace and wisdom, I ask that my prayers be answered. Amen.

March 25

For I, the Lord your God, hold your right hand; it is I who say to you, "Do not fear, I will help you."
—Isaiah 41:13

*W*henever I feel as though I don't know which way to turn or what choice to make, I know, dear God, that I can stop, take a deep breath, and listen for you to speak to me in gentle tones. For that is your voice, God, telling me which direction to go, and you have never been wrong. I know sometimes I don't listen, or maybe I try my own way first and fail, but in the end, your guidance always leads me down the righteous path to where your blessings await me.

We know our journey is safe because the Lord gives us confidence as we move to where he is calling us.

 # March 26

> *Without faith it is impossible to please God, for whoever*
> *would approach him must believe that he exists*
> *and that he rewards those who seek him.*
>
> —Hebrews 11:6

*L*ord, again today I had a conversation with someone who seems to be putting her faith into all the wrong things. Yes, her life may be improved temporarily by a different diet or another exercise program, but if those things are all she has, Lord, she is missing out on so much more. She may even find inspiration in some of the self-help books she buys, but in the end, she can't find meaning in herself alone. Thank you, Lord, that you make yourself available to all who are willing to put their faith in you. Please reach my friend, and give her the courage to believe in you.

Faith is neither proven through logic nor
reason; it must be felt with the heart.

March 27

Blessed be the God and Father of our Lord Jesus Christ, the Father of mercies and the God of all consolation, who consoles us in all our affliction, so that we may be able to console those who are in any affliction with the consolation with which we ourselves are consoled by God.

—2 Corinthians 1:3–4

God, give me a caring heart filled with compassion for all living things. Help me understand the suffering of others, that I might find a way to support them in their darkest hours. Teach me to reach out with open arms and a welcoming heart and to embrace those who are in need of warmth and comfort. Show me, dear Lord, how to have mercy on others, as you have graciously shown your mercy to me. Let me be a blessing to those I come in contact with and a shelter in the storms of their lives. Amen.

March 28

This is the boldness we have in him, that if we ask anything according to his will, he hears us. And if we know that he hears us in whatever we ask, we know that we have obtained the requests made of him.
—1 John 5:14–15

*F*ather, I have not always been strong in my faith. During those times, difficult circumstances have dragged me down, and I tend to look at myself rather than look to you for strength and courage. But as I turn my heart back in your direction, dear Lord, I once again begin to see how I am constantly and eternally blessed and how my faith is what brings your good into my life. Without faith, I have nothing. With faith—my faith in you—I have everything I could ever want and more. Amen.

Faith is the force of life.
— Leo Tolstoy

March 29

*See if I will not open the windows of heaven for you
and pour down for you an overflowing blessing.*

—Malachi 3:10

$\mathcal{D}$ear Lord, I know you don't ask us to tithe just so we can experience your blessings, but I also know you are most likely to shower them upon us when we are walking in obedience and giving a generous part of our income. I don't ever want to displease you with my finances. Please accept all that I offer to you, Lord, as well as all that I am. I stand ready to give with a cheerful heart while receiving the outpouring of your blessings. I pray with a grateful heart and in Jesus' precious name. Amen.

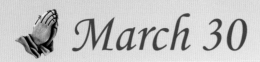

March 30

Even though I walk through the darkest valley, I fear no evil; for you are with me; your rod and your staff—they comfort me.

—Psalm 23:4

*G*od, I am hurting today. All the wounds I've received in this lifetime seem open and raw, and only the balm of your love can comfort me. I need you to take me in your loving hands, fill me with your Holy Spirit, and ease all the aching, lonely places as only you can. I know that your power is endless and your love is merciful, and I have faith in your all-healing presence. I pray that all my worries and cares will be washed away from me, just as my sins were taken from me by the sacrifice of your Son, Jesus Christ. Amen.

He is a loving, tender hand, full of sympathy and compassion.

— Dwight L. Moody

March 31

For I will proclaim the name of the Lord;
ascribe greatness to our God!
—Deuteronomy 32:3

*D*ear heavenly Father, without you my life would be
aimless and meaningless, but because of the hope
you've planted in my heart, I can rejoice even when
I'm experiencing hardship and grief. The hope you've
given me is like the beacon in a dense fog, for it guides
me to my eternal destination. Because of your Son,
I have an abiding hope in a future with you in your
eternal heavenly kingdom. Because of your Son,
I have an inspiring hope that I will become a far better
person than I am. Because of your Son, I have an
encouraging hope that I will always enjoy a special
intimacy with those believers whom I have come to
love. Thank you, dear Father, for blessing me with such
a hope that only Jesus Christ could give me. I pray in
his precious name. Amen.

My Prayer Life

_____

_____

_____

_____

_____

_____

_____

_____

_____

_____

_____

_____

_____

_____

_____

_____

_____

_____

_____

_____

_____

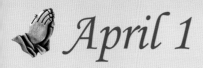 *April 1*

You came near when I called on you; you said, "Do not fear!"
You have taken up my cause, O Lord,
you have redeemed my life.
—Lamentations 3:57–58

*C*reator God, it's always amazing to see the first signs of spring. The crocuses that pop up through the snow, the bright green buds on the trees, they all catch us by surprise because we've become so accustomed to the cold and dreary days. But you, O Lord, revive us with the beauty of your creation. How good it is for us to remember that just as you protect the seeds and plants under the winter snow and bring them back to life, you also protect us in the dreariest of times! Thank you for new life in our world and in our hearts, Lord.

Renewal in the Lord brings unspeakable joy!

April 2

Revere the Lord, and serve him in sincerity
and in faithfulness.
—Joshua 24:14

$\mathcal{D}$ear God, today we ask you to send your grace in abundance to the men and women serving in our armed forces—those deployed to fight wars in foreign lands and those serving in posts within our country. Through your grace, God, help them know that they are appreciated and respected. May they sense your active presence in their lives when they are put in harm's way, and may the prayers of a grateful nation fortify them. By your grace, Lord, keep them safe, and teach them to serve with honor.

April 3

*[Bear] with one another in love, making every effort to
maintain the unity of the Spirit in the bond of peace.*
—Ephesians 4:2–3

*O*ur holy God, I need to forgive someone at my
church who has truly done harm to me and my family,
yet I cannot find it in my heart to do so. I am not an
unkind person, but I am having trouble taking the
moral high road and letting go of what was done and
the effects it had. Please show me the path to complete
forgiveness, because I know that if I don't do this, I will
end up only harming myself and damaging the unity
of our church family. Help me let go of the hurt and of
the one who hurt us, and help me move on. I pray in
Jesus' precious name. Amen.

*The greatest gift we can offer is forgiveness, for
its dual power to set the other person
free and to set us free as well.*

 *April 4*

Give thanks to the Lord of hosts; for the Lord is good,
for his steadfast love endures forever!
—Jeremiah 33:11

*G*od, when all else fails, I know that I can count on you to give me rest and help me find peace. I am grateful to know that no matter what is going on in my life, I have someone who understands and who I can lean on. Sometimes I forget, and I lash out in anger or frustration at those I love, but you forever remind me that I only need to go to you to find mercy, love, and peace. It's then that my anger and frustration disappear. Thanks be to you, God.

Prayer opens the door to peace.

April 5

You were washed, you were sanctified, you were justified in the name of the Lord Jesus Christ and in the Spirit of our God.
—1 Corinthians 6:11

*D*ear Lord, you have removed my transgressions in the blink of an eye. You grant me daily renewal in the name of your Son, Jesus Christ. You are with me always in all things. Because I have committed myself to you, I don't need to wear the sins of my past upon me or carry my mistakes with me. I can lay them at your feet, starting anew each morning. Thank you for redeeming me and allowing me to follow you. Amen.

The grace of the living God gives our parched soul the sustenance and nourishment it needs.

April 6

I will greatly rejoice in the Lord, my whole being shall exult in my God; for he has clothed me with the garments of salvation, he has covered me with the robe of righteousness.

—Isaiah 61:10

I wear my faith draped over me like a powerful robe, dear God in heaven, that can make mountains move out of my way and part the waters before me. My faith keeps me strong and purposeful, always bringing me through the dark valleys into the sunlight again. My faith in you, loving God, is my mighty power, which I use for only the highest and the best good. I pray that my faith in you might be a beacon for others to follow, should they ever lose their own faith, to remind them that, like me, they are never without your presence or your love. Amen.

 *April 7*

So let us not grow weary in doing what is right, for we will reap at harvest time, if we do not give up.
—Galatians 6:9

*D*ear Lord, I am wracked with fear and anger. I want to lash out against those who have harmed me. I am filled with hatred so strong that you are the only one who can make it abate. I pray that you lay your hand on me and transform my animosity to love and my fear to compassion. Make me care as much about the other person as I care about myself. Remove my selfish concerns, and fill me instead with peace and kindness. This task is impossible for me without your help, but with you, all things are possible. Amen.

A life of compassion toward others is a life of reverence toward Christ.

 *April 8*

Do not store up for yourselves treasures on earth, where moth and rust consume and where thieves break in and steal, but store up for yourselves treasures in heaven, where neither moth nor rust consumes and where thieves do not break in and steal.

—Matthew 6:19–20

*H*eavenly Father, when I look back on my life, I see material possessions I'm proud of, awards I've achieved, and accolades I've won. But then I realize that nothing I have of value has come from the work of my hands. It's only through your unmerited grace that I have a life worth living. Without you and the sacrifice of your Son, Jesus Christ, I'm nothing. Please humble my heart so I may be a better Christian.

April 9

Only fear the Lord, and serve him faithfully with all your heart; for consider what great things he has done for you.
—1 Samuel 12:24

*H*eavenly Father, I admit I am sometimes very selfish and greedy and always seem to want more. You have blessed me with so much, and yet my heart still desires. Help me temper my need for more and learn to truly appreciate the things I already have. Help me see the joy in my life just the way it is right now without anything adding to it. Help me be grateful for where I am this day while doing what is right here and now. And help me enjoy the blessings of the moment. In the name of Jesus Christ, I pray. Amen.

Gratitude is a key that unlocks the door to treasures you already have, and it yields greater treasures yet to be discovered.

April 10

I will satisfy the weary, and all who are faint I will replenish.

—Jeremiah 31:25

*L*ord, I'm surrounded by a few people who are struggling through each day because, night after night, sleep eludes them. No amount of warm milk brings slumber. Even doses of sleep-inducing drugs fail to give them the blessed relief they need. Send your peaceful rest to these people, Lord. Gently close their eyes with your compassionate touch and reassure them that you who never sleep are watching over them through the night. We ask this in your precious name. Amen.

The soul is at peace when it rests in God's hands.

April 11

*May the God of hope fill you with all joy and peace
in believing, so that you may abound in
hope by the power of the Holy Spirit.*

—Romans 15:13

Almighty God, you are my hope and my salvation.
When there is only darkness, I seek your light to
remind me that one must never give up hope. Your
strength shores me up when I am weak, and your love
warms the cold spots in my heart. I suddenly find that
there is a reason to keep going and that someday all
will be well. You are my hope and my foundation. In
you, I place my faith and my trust.

*Hope helps us know that in the midst of feeling
all alone, God is still with me.*

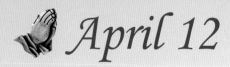 *April 12*

Blessed are those who trust in the Lord, whose trust is the Lord. They shall be like a tree planted by water, sending out its roots by the stream.

—Jeremiah 17:7–8

Lord, I don't know when I've felt this completely drained. I know you can see what a state I'm in. I feel as though I barely have enough energy to make it through the day. I'm so empty inside that I have nothing to give to the people I love. And they notice.

Fill me, Lord, as only you can. Fill me with your purpose for me, that I may be full to over-flowing—all to your glory!

God invites us to run into his protective embrace.

April 13

Rejoice in the Lord always; again I will say, Rejoice.
—Philippians 4:4

*L*ord, today as I look
around me, my heart is full
of gratitude for all the blessings of an ordinary day.
I don't take for granted the fact
that I have a roof over my head and
plenty of food for my family. I appreciate the ability to
simply fall into the routine of a busy day with no major
disasters, crises, or life-changing experiences. The
ordinary day is a precious gift, Lord, and I'm so glad
I know whom to thank for it.

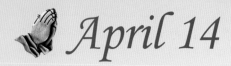 *April 14*

For God all things are possible.
—Mark 10:27

*L*ord, could you please help me love the unlovable?
I know it isn't possible for me to do this alone, so allow
me to see them through your eyes—as precious people
created in your image. I know that in some ways we all
look the same to you, Lord, even as you are so keenly
aware of our differences. To you, we are
all lovable. Give me eyes to see others
the way you do, Lord. Without
you, it's simply not possible.

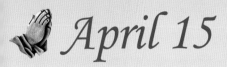# April 15

He brought me to the banqueting house,
and his intention toward me was love.
—Song of Solomon 2:4

O Lord Almighty, what comfort I find in your constancy and faithfulness. You are the same God who hung the stars in the universe and called them by name. You've heard the prayers of troubled souls since the beginning of time, and yet you never stop listening. Thank you, Lord, for your remarkable sovereignty and your unfailing love. You are indeed our comfort and our strength when all about us seems to be falling apart. Amen.

God never stops telling us, "I love you."

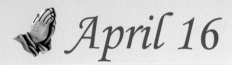 *April 16*

If I take the wings of the morning and settle at the farthest limits of the sea, even there your hand shall lead me, and your right hand shall hold me fast.

—Psalm 139:9–10

*D*ear Lord, why would I ever think I could escape your guidance in my life and why would I want to? There have been times, Lord, when I knew you were telling me to make a difficult phone call, offer up an apology, or let go of an unhealthy goal, and I pretended that I didn't hear you. Please forgive my stubbornness and my pride, Lord, for I know that if I didn't have your leading in my life, I would take many wrong turns. Thank you for seeking me out, no matter where I might try to hide and for patiently waiting for me to see things your way, which is the best way.

Remember to turn to God for help, for in him there is rescue, refuge, and peace.

 *April 17*

There is no fear in love, but perfect love casts out fear.
—1 John 4:18

*F*ather, because you have forgiven me, you have removed all fear from my life. I no longer need to worry about what challenges I will encounter. At the end of the day, I can return to you, secure in the knowledge that all my transgressions and sins will be washed away. Each day my slate is wiped clean, giving me another chance to live a life according to your will and purpose. Let me be worthy of this precious gift.

If we trust in the Lord and ask his forgiveness, he will bless us with mercy and peace.

April 18

The blessing of the Lord makes rich,
and he adds no sorrow with it.
—Proverbs 10:22

Lord, it amazes me to see how your compassion falls generously and equally on those who believe in you and honor you and on those who do not. How narrow-minded it is of us to think that your blessings are only for those who have surrendered their lives to you! Thank you for including us all in your compassion, Lord. The life-giving rain, the heartwarming sunshine, and all your many blessings are generously distributed—and we thank and praise you for that compassion.

Joy excludes none, for God's love invites us all.

April 19

For the grace of God has appeared, bringing salvation to all.
—Titus 2:11

Amazing Grace, how sweet the sound,

That saved a wretch like me.

I once was lost but now am found,

Was blind, but now I see.

'Twas Grace that taught my heart to fear.

And Grace, my fears relieved.

How precious did that Grace appear

The hour I first believed.

Through many dangers, toils and snares

I have already come;

'Tis Grace that brought me safe thus far

and Grace will lead me home.

—John Newton, "Amazing Grace"

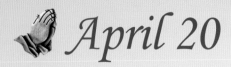 *April 20*

*Take the shield of faith, with which you will be able to quench
all the flaming arrows of the evil one.*

—Ephesians 6:16

*H*eavenly Father, I have discovered that when my faith seems in short supply, I can still trust you, and then my faith actually grows. When I find myself falling into the pattern of ruminating and obsessing over the details of how a particular circumstance will work out, I remind myself to turn to you, and suddenly I find my faith becomes strong again. Thank you for these little ways in which you strengthen my relationship with you. With all my heart, I love you.

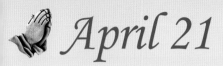

April 21

*For a child has been born for us, a son given to us . . .
and he is named Wonderful Counselor, Mighty
God, Everlasting Father, Prince of Peace.*

—Isaiah 9:6

*A*lmighty God, how blessed we are that when you chose to send your Son to earth it was not as the prince of power and domination, but as the Prince of Peace! You knew we would need his peace both as nations populating the earth and in the innermost places of our hearts. Hear our voices lifted up in gratitude, O God! We are a people who could not survive without the Prince of Peace in our lives. Thank you for your indescribable gift.

True peace comes from the Lord.

April 22

He said to them, "Why are you afraid, you of little faith?"
Then he got up and rebuked the winds and the
seas; and there was a dead calm.

—Matthew 8:26

*G*od, you are my rock and my foundation. When the
storms of life rage around me, I know that I can seek
warmth and security in your loving grace. You are a
beacon guiding me through the thick fog of fear and
confusion to the safe comfort of the shore. Steady and
true are your love and your strength. Steadfast and
secure am I in the light of your changeless and timeless
presence that permeates the darkest of dark nights.

His presence comforts me and gives me the
courage to keep going no matter
what the circumstances.

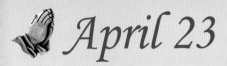 *April 23*

*God, the Lord, is my strength; he makes my feet like the feet of
a deer, and makes me tread upon the heights.*
—Habakkuk 3:19

*H*oly One, blessed is your name! Because nothing
can separate me from your love, I have peace beyond
all human understanding. The cares of this world are
meaningless, because I can rest fully in the knowledge
that you are watching over me, protecting me, and
helping me. You are the light and
the life, and your love is
eternal. Praise be to God,
for it is through your Son
that I am saved. Amen.

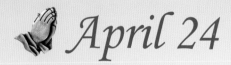

April 24

Whoever wishes to become great among you must be your servant.

—Mark 10:43

My wonderful Lord, today I ask you to bless all the physicians, nurses, and other medical personnel who work so tirelessly to care for others. Good health is one of the greatest blessings you give us, Lord—we know that for sure. When we aren't well, we truly appreciate the expertise and the caring hands of those you send to minister to us. So bless them, Lord. Extend to them an extra dose of appreciation today. And please give them times to rest.

When we give thanks and praise to someone, we honor the presence of God in that person.

April 25

Therefore I tell you, do not worry about your life, what you
will eat or what you will drink, or about your body,
what you will wear. Is not life more than food,
and the body more than clothing?
—Matthew 6:25

My Lord, my mind is often overcome with anxiety
and worry, but you have told us over and over again
that you want us to place our trust and hope in you.
Please help me release my worries about the future
and instead turn to you for all things. I can't
control anything except the direction of
my thoughts, and I want those to be
one continuous prayer of thanks
and praise to you. I make my
request in your holy name.

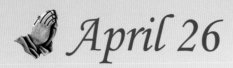# *April 26*

Therefore we have been buried with him by baptism into death, so that, just as Christ was raised from the dead by the glory of the Father, so we too might walk in newness of life.

—Romans 6:4

*D*ear Lord, you have come to save us and make us new again in Christ. When we are baptized in your name, we can cast off our old life, like removing a dirty, stained shirt. We emerge, renewed, cloaked in sparkling robes that shine more brightly than the sun. Our sins are washed away, and we are free from our past. Please remind me that I can have that renewal of spirit at any time, just by praying to you and accepting your forgiveness. I ask in your name. Amen.

Let's remember to pray and ask God to help us discover renewed joy.

# *April 27*

Now the Lord is the Spirit, and where the Spirit
of the Lord is, there is freedom.
—2 Corinthians 3:17

*O*God, some of my friends and family members don't understand why I'm constantly looking to you for direction in my life. They see my faith in you as something restrictive and limiting, but if they only knew that following after you actually sets my heart free. You don't restrict me with your will in my life. Rather you lead me to where I can be the most fruitful, the most fulfilled, and the most like you. Give me a soft heart toward those who don't understand the many blessings in following your guidance, for unless they see your benefits through the way I live my life, they may not have an opportunity to see them at all.

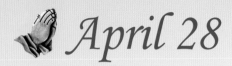

April 28

The Lord God helps me; therefore I have not been disgraced;
therefore I have set my face like flint, and I know that I shall
not be put to shame; he who vindicates me is near.
—Isaiah 50:7–8

*F*orgive me, Lord, for all my mistakes and my sins.
I try my best, but I often fall short of the goals I set for
myself, and though I know I am only human, I long to
be perfect in your eyes. Please show me the lessons I
need to learn from my mistakes, and also show me how
I can make amends to anyone I have harmed today
and in the past. I want to free my own heart of the
turmoil of resentment and thus free them from my
anger as well. Forgive me, Lord, for falling short, and
help me aim higher next time.

April 29

This is his commandment, that we should believe in the name of his Son Jesus Christ and love one another, just as he has commanded us.

—1 John 3:23

*L*ord, thank you for sending Jesus Christ to show us how to live. Through his life, death, and rebirth, you demonstrated not only the depths of your dedication to us, but you also provided a concrete example to the world of how to live as a complete expression of love. Thank you for giving us your beloved Son, so that we, too, can have eternal life. We pray in Jesus' holy name. Amen.

Were there no God, we would be in this glorious world with grateful hearts: and no one to thank.

—Christina Georgina Rossetti

April 30

You who have done great things, O God, who is like you? You who have made me see many troubles and calamities will revive me again; from the depths of the earth you will bring me up again. You will increase my honor, and comfort me once again.

—Psalm 71:19–21

I feel an old familiar panic coming over me, Lord. Comfort me now! As I breathe deeply, fill me with the knowledge that you are present and you are in control. Thank you, Lord. Only your intervention can calm my troubled soul.

You restore me with strength and hope and the courage to face a new day.

My Prayer Life

_____
_____
_____
_____
_____
_____
_____
_____
_____
_____
_____
_____
_____
_____
_____
_____
_____
_____
_____
_____
_____

 *May 1*

*Again, truly I tell you, if two of you agree on earth about
anything you ask, it will be done for you by my Father
in heaven. For where two or three are gathered
in my name, I am there among them.*
—Matthew 18:19–20

*M*y Lord and Savior, today I thank you for your holy
church. What a blessing it is to be able to join together
in worship and praise for you, sharing our love for
Jesus with other believers! Gathering with this community has filled my spirit over and over again. When my
energy is lagging or my heart is heavy, my brothers and
sisters in Christ help me carry my burden, and
suddenly I feel light again. Thank you for
blessing us with each other.

God is the tie that binds us all together.

 *May 2*

I will make them strong in the Lord, and they
shall walk in his name, says the Lord.
—Zechariah 10:12

*D*ear God, it's hard to keep the faith when I see everything around me falling apart. I know that faith is belief in things unseen, but I find it difficult to hold on to the unseen when what I see is causing me so much trouble. Help me find the courage to get through this. I have faith in you and want to have faith in myself to meet any challenges I encounter. Please, Lord, if I get weak, help me lean on you for a while until I am strong enough to rise up and do what needs to be done. I think that together we can do anything, God. I put my faith in you. Amen.

When we offer ourselves openly,
he will always answer.

 *May 3*

Peace I leave with you; my peace I give to you. I do not give to you as the world gives. Do not let your hearts be troubled, and do not let them be afraid.
—John 14:27

Lord, so often my mind knows a situation will work out for good, but my heart is full of fear. Or my heart believes, but my mind races through the night with all the "what ifs" and "shoulds" that so often direct my steps. I need your peace, Lord, in both my heart and mind. May your peace be pervasive in me, so that my first response to any situation will come from a place of peace and not a place of panic. Thank you, Lord.

May 4

I, I am He who blots out your transgressions for my own sake, and I will not remember your sins.

—Isaiah 43:25

Holy God, I am praying for forgiveness—not from you, but from the one I hurt. I acted thoughtlessly, perhaps even maliciously, and I have harmed that person. I have already received your forgiveness by coming to you in penitence, but I need to seek forgiveness from the person I hurt, and I am afraid he will not accept my apology. Give me strength to admit my wrongdoing to him, and I ask that you will soften his heart toward me. I know I was wrong. I do not deserve forgiveness, but I pray that he will have mercy on me as you have mercy on me.

May 5

I am the Lord; I act with steadfast love, justice, and
righteousness in the earth, for in these
things I delight, says the Lord.
—Jeremiah 9:24

*W*hat is God's grace? It is the breath of God upon
my face and the touch of God upon my heart, gently
moving me in the right direction. What is God's grace?
It is the whisper of love in my ear and the comfort of
warmth on my skin, promising that the cold, dark
nights will come to an end. What is God's grace? It is
the laughter of a child and the hugs of a friend, lifting
my spirit ever higher. What is God's grace? It is the
presence of God, who is kind, good, and loving and
to whom I can always turn.

We are blessed because of God's grace.

 *May 6*

As the Father has loved me, so I have loved you; abide in my love. If you keep my commandments, you will abide in my love, . . . I am giving you these commands so that you may love one another.
—John 15:9–10, 17

*L*ove is the highest calling, God, and you have called me today to find love where there is only strife and confusion. You have asked me to rise to the challenge of loving those in my life who may not deserve it and to give love to those who may not believe it is real. Let me act in your honor, God, spreading the love I feel to anyone who needs it. Love is the gift that keeps on giving, and I have plenty of love to give. Amen.

When we get in touch with his powerful, everlasting love for us, it overflows to others.

May 7

Happy is everyone who fears the Lord, who walks in his ways.
You shall eat the fruit of the labor of your hands;
you shall be happy, and it shall go well with you.
—Psalm 128:1–2

*S*ometimes I'm impatient, God. I want what I want when I want it, and I get tired of waiting for good to manifest in my life. But I know that I should persevere and that I should release my wants and needs to your divine timing. I also know that if I keep my heart focused on hope rather than on what I lack, I will be filled with the goodness you have intended for me. Help me, God, to slow down, relax, and surrender to your time clock. You alone know what is best for me and when it is best for me to have it.

May 8

For everything created by God is good.
—1 Timothy 4:4

*T*here she is, Lord, that little cat that you brought into my life—one of your most endearing creatures for sure. How relaxing it is to stroke her soft fur as she curls up in my lap! How much I can learn from her about making time to play—and about finding the sunniest spots in life! You have blessed us with pets to make our hearts glad and to be our companions through the sunshine and the rain. We don't want to forget to thank you, Lord, for them. We're so glad you took the time to create them, for they make our lives far richer.

Pets love without strings and share the simplest joys, slowing me to a pace that God affirms.

 *May 9*

*Do not judge, so that you may not be judged. For with
the judgment you make you will be judged, and the
measure you give will be the measure you get.*
—Matthew 7:1–2

*H*eavenly Father, it's so much easier to criticize
others for their faults than to turn the focus inward.
I am guilty of being judgmental and of acting as if
I know better how to mete out justice and discipline
than you in all your wisdom and mercy. I pray that you
will help me have compassion for my fellow humans
and help me realize that the only person I can really
change is me. I need to let go of my judgments and
harshness and treat others with loving kindness. I know
I need to work on my own shortcomings. I ask for help
in your name. Amen.

 # *May 10*

*Let us run with perseverance the race that is set before us,
looking to Jesus the pioneer and perfector of our faith.*
—Hebrews 12:1–2

God, this marathon of life sometimes leaves my feet
sore and aching. But with the grace of your everlasting
love, I know that I will be given new strength to lift me
up and carry me along when my feet just cannot go
on. You have always been there for me, and I know
that you will always be there for me now, even when it
appears that I am on my own. All I need to do is look
within and I will see that I have someone running this
marathon alongside me, offering a
helping hand and an encouraging
word when I think I cannot take
one more step.

# May 11

*Strive first for the kingdom of God and his righteousness,
and all these things will be given to you as well.*
—Matthew 6:33

*H*eavenly Father, it's hard to resist the temptations of this world. Material goods, false glory, and temporary fame are all held in front of me and revered by those around me. I know these things do not hold lasting meaning and that they are only false idols used by your enemy to tempt me into forsaking you. Though I realize they are mirages, I still am susceptible to their lure. Please help me remain strong and seek only you and the things that are lasting and true. By relying only on you to guide my steps, I can have all that my heart desires. I ask in your holy name.

*Faith perceives a truth that lies beyond
our field of vision—a truth only
our heart has eyes to see.*

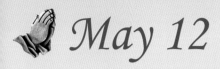

May 12

Sing to the Lord; praise the Lord!
For he has delivered the life of the needy.
—Jeremiah 20:13

*S*ometimes a light surprises

the child of God who sings;

it is the Lord who rises

with healing in his wings.

When comforts are declining,

God grants the soul again

a season of clear shining,

to cheer it after rain.
—William Cowper, "Sometimes a Light Surprises"

We are emboldened and renewed
by his everlasting love.

# May 13

I know, O Lord, that your judgments are right, and that in faithfulness you have humbled me. Let your steadfast love become my comfort according to your promise to your servant.
—Psalm 119:75–76

*L*ord, love seems really difficult sometimes. The ones I love often hurt me, and I am sure I am not always kind to them either. Help me understand them better and be kinder and more compassionate when they push my buttons and try my patience. I want to be a loving person, but I don't always feel so loving. I pray for the strength and patience to always choose love over anger, peace over turmoil. Thank you, dear God.

 # *May 14*

Now to him who by the power at work within us is able to
accomplish abundantly far more than all we can ask
or imagine, to him be glory in the church and in
Christ Jesus to all generations, forever and ever.
—Ephesians 3:20–21

*L*ord, I sometimes feel I am not worthy of all the
good you have given me. But I know that you love all
your children equally, and I am honored to be the
recipient of your bountiful blessings. I look around me
each day and am in awe of how much you have given
me, not just in material things, but also the people
you have chosen to enter my life. I am grateful for the
lessons I've learned, even though many of them were
learned the hard way. Thank you for continuing to
bless me with even more good things, and I promise to
choose to do all I can to be worthy of them. Amen.

God's protective love is a praiseworthy blessing.

 *May 15*

*Everyone who drinks of this water will be thirsty again,
but those who drink of the water that I will give them will
never be thirsty. The water that I will give will become
in them a spring of water gushing up to eternal life.*
—John 4:13–14

*D*ear Father, please hear my prayer and guide me through my decisions and desires. I have faith and hope, but I could use more. I have gratitude, but I could use more. I'm not perfect, but I'm trying to be, and I could use more help in the form of grace when I make horrible mistakes. Teach me to take things in stride, learn the lessons the first time around, and have patience and tolerance for those who test my spirit. Lord, I could use more of the living waters you have to give me.

May 16

Wretched man that I am! Who will rescue me from this body of death? Thanks be to God through Jesus Christ our Lord!
—Romans 7:24–25

*S*overeign Father, I know you have already forgiven me, but I cannot find that same compassion for myself. I keep going over and over my errors and transgressions, allowing them to fester in my soul as I am shrouded in shame. I have sinned repeatedly, despite my longing to follow your commandments. Please take this burden of shame and embarrassment from me, wrapping me instead in your mercy and love. Let me be free from self-judgment as I continue to move closer to the life you envision for me.

 *May 17*

Be subject to one another out of reverence for Christ.
—Ephesians 5:21

*L*ord, it seems as if so many marriages are in need of renewal. I come to you today to ask for your intervention in troubled marriages. Restore husbands and wives to the positions of respect and love you want them to have, Lord. Allow them to see one another through your eyes and to remember all the reasons they fell in love in the first place. Reignite the fires of romance, Lord! This world is hard on marriage, but you created it for the people you love, and only you can make it as rich and rewarding as you intended it to be. Give us an abiding love for each other. Teach us to cherish the marriages you ordained. Amen.

 *May 18*

*Consider the ravens: they neither sow nor reap, they have
neither storehouse nor barn, and yet God feeds them.
Of how much more value are you then the birds!*

—Luke 12:24

$\mathscr{P}$recious Lord, today I want to thank you for the blessing of having just enough—not too much and not too little, but just what's needed for my family and me. Whether it is food to eat, clothing to wear, a roof over our heads, or any of the opportunities you offer us, we will never stop thanking you for your provision. In your wisdom and mercy, you have not given us abundantly more than we need so that we might become obsessed with material things. Nor have you given us so little that we might have to focus all our energies and resources on our survival. Instead, you've given us just enough, and we acknowledge that perfect provision for the complete blessing that it is.

May 19

Happy are those whose help is the God of Jacob, whose hope is in the Lord their God, who made heaven and earth, the sea, and all that is in them; who keeps faith forever; who executes justice for the oppressed; who gives food to the hungry.

—Psalm 146:5–7

*H*oly Father, you reward those whose hope is in you. Please remind me to rely only on you in times of trouble and to turn to you as a first resort instead of a last resort. No problem of mine is too great for you to solve, dear Lord, nor is any problem too small to escape your notice. You can do anything, and your will is sovereign. I put myself in your hands, today, tomorrow, and forever.

If we trust in God's goodness, he will bring us comfort and restore our hope in the future.

 # May 20

I have said this to you, so that in me you may have peace.
In the world you face persecution. But take courage;
I have conquered the world!
—John 16:33

*L*ord, in the midst of the least peaceful situation imaginable, I want to reflect your peace. I ask you to open my heart so that I can feel your peace in the midst of chaos and confusion. And once I find it, Lord, please use your holy power to enable your peace to shine through me into the lives of others. I want to be a reflection of the kind of calm and peace that can only come from you. Use me, Lord. In the midst of chaos, please use me.

 *May 21*

The Lord is my rock, my fortress, and my deliverer.
—2 Samuel 22:2

*L*ord, when all else fails I know that I can count on you to be my fortress and my foundation. I give thanks each day for the steadfast comfort you provide, and I pray that you will give this same comfort to those who suffer in fear and silence today. Give to them the same freedom from worry as you have me, by showing them the same mercy and love you show me each day. Be their fortress just as you are mine so that they, too, may understand that they need never walk alone.

In the presence of our compassion,
Christ is made more meaningful to others.

 *May 22*

*For my thoughts are not your thoughts, nor are your ways my
ways, says the Lord. For as the heavens are higher than
the earth, so are my ways higher than your ways
and my thoughts than your thoughts.*
—Isaiah 55:8–9

*D*ear Father in heaven, I am thankful that whenever
I don't know what to say or do, I can turn to you in
prayer and find the answers that I need. Your guidance
has never led me down the wrong path, and it always
calls for me to do the best in any situation. When I
listen to my own advice, things don't always turn out
well, but your advice is tried and true and truly divine.
They say that Father knows best, and I agree. Your
wisdom always takes me right where I need to be. I
pray in the name of your precious Son, Jesus. Amen.

May 23

*Whenever you stand praying, forgive, if you have anything
against anyone; so that your Father in heaven
may also forgive you your trespasses.*
—Mark 11:25

*M*y supreme Lord, give me a forgiving heart. When
someone unintentionally ignores me or hurts my
feelings, let me respond with forgiveness before they
are even aware of the wrong. In these and other
situations, I pray that forgiveness will become an
automatic response for me and not something I have
to consciously work on. I guess what I'm really asking,
Lord, is please give me a heart like yours. Only then
will I be able to live a life full of spontaneous
forgiveness.

*God's forgiving grace can touch and change us
and extend to others through our example.*

May 24

*You are a hiding place for me; you preserve me from trouble;
you surround me with glad cries of deliverance.*

—Psalm 32:7

O Lord, how often I turn to you when I don't know where else to turn! If only I would always turn to you first. My faith in you is a constant in my life, and yet too often I let other influences distract me and lead me away from a total reliance on you. I know in my heart that it is in you, and you only, that I'm protected and safe. Please shelter me, Lord! You are the only place I want to run to in times of trouble. My faith rests entirely in you.

*Faith is leaning on the only one
who is able to hold me up.*

May 25

I will walk among you, and will be your God,
and you shall be my people.
—Leviticus 26:12

*H*eavenly Father, you know my shortcomings and faults. You know where I'm susceptible to temptation and where I act rashly. I pray daily that you will direct me in all things. Prevent me from leaving your path and being lost to you. Please help me be strong instead of weak, wise instead of foolish, and kind instead of cruel. Keep me far from evil, and guide me to be more like your only Son, Jesus Christ.

The Lord will set us on a true course
that will bring us closer to him.

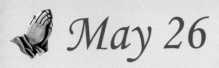# May 26

He has shown strength with his arm; he has scattered the proud in the thoughts of their hearts. He has brought down the powerful from their thrones, and lifted up the lowly.
—Luke 1:51–52

*H*eavenly Father, it all seems overwhelming: the famines, the floods, the wars, and the poverty. I feel that if I let the door to my heart open even a crack, the pain of the world will flood in, and I will be carried away by grief. So instead, I bar the door and focus on my own little world, ignoring the suffering of others. But by ignoring them, I become a participant in the sins being committed against them. Please help me bear the hurts of others, be a witness to their pain, and hold them in love and compassion. While I may not be strong enough to do this on my own, I know that with your guidance I can help ease their burdens and still carry my own. Amen.

# May 27

As for me and my household, we will serve the Lord.
—Joshua 24:15

*T*oday I will put my faith in the Lord and let his love fill me with light. I will walk lightly, talk lightly, and live lightly, letting all that is good be my guide. On new-found wings I will soar, and with newfound hope I will give of myself to anyone who needs my help today. The love of the Lord cleanses me, making me a bright reflection of his goodness. May the Lord continue to renew me and restore to me the glory he intends me to have. May I be the blessing he intended me to be to everyone I meet.

Each choice to embrace joy renews the heart.

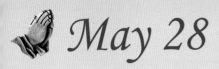# May 28

Although you have not seen him, you love him; and even though you do not see him now, you believe in him and rejoice with an indescribable and glorious joy.

—1 Peter 1:8

*D*ear God, your heavenly grace has rescued me from the darkness and brought me into the light again. Each time I'm reminded of your miraculous presence in my life, the light gets brighter and problems melt away. I know then that you have touched me with a special, loving grace that makes my heart sing out with joy just to be alive. Knowing that you deem me worthy of your grace renews my strength and hope that all will be well in my life. Thank you, God.

By opening ourselves to God's ever-present grace, our hearts sing out in joyful gratitude.

# May 29

*Enjoy life with the wife whom you love, all the days
of your vain life that are given you under the sun.*

—Ecclesiastes 9:9

Almighty God, I honestly don't know how a marriage survives without forgiveness. In fact, maybe the marriages without it don't survive. Thank you for a forgiving husband, Lord. Because he forgives me so often, it's much easier for me to forgive him when he does something thoughtless. Forgiveness prevents the weeds from taking root in a relationship and provides an environment where love can grow. Bless our marriage, Lord, and keep it well watered with forgiveness.

 *May 30*

Wait for the Lord; be strong, and let your heart take courage; wait for the Lord!
—Psalm 27:14

$\mathcal{D}$ear heavenly Father, you have commanded us to act in love at all times. I want to obey you, but I'm struggling. I am empty and tired, short of patience and forgiveness. I need an extra dose of your strength to help me. All good things come from and through you, and I know with your help I can go beyond myself and reach a new reservoir of love within me. As I face the challenges in my life today, please be with me, reminding me that with you all things are possible. Amen.

Your love enfolds me in arms so strong that I lack for nothing.

 *May 31*

Happy is the one who listens to me, watching daily at my gates, waiting beside my doors. For whoever finds me finds life and obtains favor from the Lord.
—Proverbs 8:34–35

God, I know that lately all I have been doing is praying and asking for things, complaining about what I don't have and experiencing the sadness of what I have lost. Please don't think I'm not grateful for your presence in my life. I am truly grateful. It's just that sometimes life challenges my gratitude, and I have to come back to you and talk with you. It is only then that my heart and mind can become quiet and I can remember that I already have all I need...in you.

Thou who has given so much to me, give me one thing more: a grateful heart.
—George Herbert

My Prayer Life

_____

_____

_____

_____

_____

_____

_____

_____

_____

_____

_____

_____

_____

_____

_____

_____

_____

_____

_____

_____

_____

_____

_____

_____

 *June 1*

Happy are those who live in your house,
ever singing your praise.
—Psalm 84:4

*D*ear God, thank you for teaching me that praising you is a blessing to me. How wise you are to request and graciously accept our praise, no matter how it is delivered! Not everyone can sing well, but to you it's all a joyful noise. Let us praise you with our lips and with our lives as long as we live. And, Lord, how I look forward to the day when I'm part of that great cloud of witnesses praising you face to face! I glorify you, my great Lord! Amen.

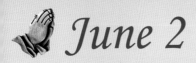 # June 2

We have this hope, a sure and steadfast anchor of the soul.
—Hebrews 6:19

Dear God, you've given us so much more than we need. Too often we get caught up in the desire to acquire, but you patiently wait for us to see the difference between a need and a want. We may long for a better job, a bigger house, or a family vacation to an exotic location. But eventually, God, we realize that all we need is you. Everything else we possess can be taken from us in a heartbeat. Indeed, we can never lose the hope that is in our souls because of you. That hope anchors us when the storms come and the winds of change gust through our lives. Thank you for the enduring hope that only comes from you.

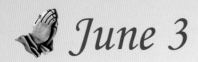 *June 3*

*Trust in the Lord with all your heart,
and do not rely on your own insight.*

—Proverbs 3:5

Lord Jesus, your peace is far from me today. I feel
separated, with all my calm leaking from broken
places. I have no patience, even for those whom I love
the most. Please lay your hand upon me, lending me
some of your strength and stillness, so I may pass it on
to others in my life. Heal my worry and still my unrest,
so that I may be filled only with thoughts of your
goodness and might.

*Those who wait patiently for God's
direction find inner peace.*

 # June 4

Jesus answered them, "Truly I tell you, if you have faith and do not doubt, not only will you do what has been done to the fig tree, but even if you say to this mountain, 'Be lifted up and thrown into the sea,' it will be done."
—Matthew 21:21

*D*ear Lord, my faith is hard to come by these days. I struggle to hold on to the little faith I have when times become as trying as they have been lately. That is why I turn to you today in prayer, because in the past you have always restored my lost faith when I wavered and weakened during the trials I was facing. I know that when I call upon you, my prayers will always be answered and a strong and fresh dose of faith will be delivered to me right away. For this I am grateful, Lord. Amen.

Each prayer is a message of faith in God.

 *June 5*

By this everyone will know that you are my disciples,
if you have love for one another.
—John 13:35

Lord, I know I need to forgive someone who wronged me. The problem is, I can't honestly say I want to forgive her. For some reason I enjoy telling myself that I was right and she was wrong. Convict me, Lord! Don't let me allow this prideful feeling to fester any longer for my own selfish satisfaction. Give me your strength to forgive so that we can put this behind us. Restore our relationship in the light of forgive-ness. Amen.

 *June 6*

> *The testing of your faith produces endurance; and let*
> *endurance have its full effect, so that you may be*
> *mature and complete, lacking in nothing.*
>
> —James 1:3–4

*L*ord, how easy it is to express gratitude when times are good, but how difficult it can be for us to also thank you for the hard times—especially when we are in the midst of them. That's not wise, Lord, and we are sorry. For when we look back over all the ups and downs of our lives, we see that you were in fact working all things together for good. For lessons learned in the hard times and for the strength you gave us to get through them, we give you thanks. After all, how can we not be grateful for something that brings us closer to you? So thank you, Lord, for the hard times.

Hardship helps us recognize God's blessings.

 # June 7

Be merciful, just as your Father is merciful.
—Luke 6:36

I am hurt and angry today, Lord. Someone I love has trampled on my heart and sinned against me, and I'm not sure what to do about it. I know I should love them anyway, but that doesn't really come easily. Thank you, Lord, for teaching us that it is possible to love the sinner even when we hate the sin. You love me in spite of all my sins and imperfections, so with your help I will try to do the same. In my heart I know there's no better response than love. May it flow freely from me today, Lord. Amen.

# June 8

Have mercy on some who are wavering.
—Jude 22

Lord, of all the gifts you have given me, I think that compassion is the greatest. My friends are always thanking me for my ability to understand their suffering. To be there for them and really hear them is the best gift I can give them. I learned that from you— from the compassion you have shown me no matter what was happening in my life. Through the lessons you teach, may I continue to go out into the world and teach others by example. Your compassion becomes mine, and I hope to be a beacon of light, love, and hope for others by your example, God.

Today, I long to pass along peace and joy and somehow resurrect hope in weary hearts.

 *June 9*

Blessed are those who mourn, for they will be comforted.
—Matthew 5:4

*O*Lord of all, only you know how deeply I am grieving. There are days when I don't know if I can catch my breath, let alone face my responsibilities with a clear mind and a willing spirit. Come into my pain, Lord. Begin your miraculous healing from the inside out, because without you, I honestly don't know how I'll get through this. Send your comfort, Lord, and caress me with your compassion.

Through the darkest days, God walks beside us.

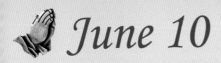# June 10

For the Lord is good; his steadfast love endures forever,
and his faithfulness to all generations.
—Psalm 100:5

*H*eavenly Father, if ever we need your wise intervention and guidance, it's in the rearing of our precious children. Just when we think we have them figured out, they reach another stage of development, and we're left feeling totally inadequate all over again. Be the good and wise Father of us all. Give us your insight, your compassion, and your creativity so that we can navigate the child-rearing years with your grace for the benefit of our children. Most of all, dear Father, soften our children's hearts so they will know how hard we are trying and how very much we love them. We pray in the name of your beloved Son. Amen.

 *June 11*

I will rejoice in the Lord;
I will exult in the God of my salvation.
—Habakkuk 3:18

Almighty God, how sweet your amazing grace is to my soul! Like a healing balm from above, you soothe my fears and comfort my anxious heart. Your presence is a candle that no wind can blow out. Your wondrous grace is ever-present and is an infinite light that guides me always to you. When your grace appears in my life, I know that I am always cared for and watched over by the one who loves me most. Your sweet, amazing grace is the gift of your love—a love that knows no boundaries or limitations.

His grace fills me with the strength
I need to move through this day.

# June 12

Two are better than one, because they have a good reward for their toil. For if they fall, one will lift up the other; but woe to one who is alone and falls and does not have another to help.
—Ecclesiastes 4:9–10

*L*ord, there are times when it's easy for me to love the people I share my life with and times when it's just so hard. On the difficult days, Lord, I pray that you would help me love as you love. I come to you to draw on your unending source of pure love, so that I can let my first response to any situation be a response based not on my own self-interest, but based on love. Thank you, Lord, for loving us. If you didn't, we'd never be able to love others in a way that brings you glory.

By spreading the joy of his love, we improve the lives of those around us—and our own lives in the process.

 *June 13*

My Lord, I long to know my purpose in life. I love being who I am right now and the roles you have given me to play, but there is an ache inside of me that can be filled only by being of service to others. Please guide me to the path that was destined for me at birth so that I can be the best person I can be. I'm happy with all you have given me, but now I want to give back. Guide me to the best way possible to do that, Lord.

June 14

God lives in us, and his love is perfected in us.

—1 John 4:12

*J*esus, thou art all compassion,

pure, unbounded love thou art;

Visit us with thy salvation,

enter ev'ry trembling heart.

Breathe, O breathe thy loving Spirit

into ev'ry troubled breast;

Let us all in thee inherit,

let us find thy promised rest.

Take away our bent to sinning,

Alpha and Omega be;

End of faith, as its beginning,

set our hearts at liberty.

—Charles Wesley,
"Love Divine, All Loves Excelling"

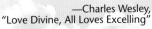

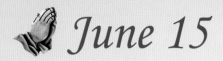

June 15

Thanks be to God, who in Christ always leads us in triumphal procession, and through us spreads in every place the fragrance that comes from knowing him.

—2 Corinthians 2:14

Lord, everything around me is a miracle and a gift from you. Each blade of grass, the laugh of a baby, the wind in the trees...they are all created by you. Even the challenges I come across are lessons for me to help me grow in spirit and become more Christlike in my thoughts and actions. Thank you for every experience, because when I approach each relationship and opportunity with your guidance, I move further along my journey toward you. I thank you. Amen.

How good it is to bask in the warmth of his love!

 # June 16

They are not afraid of evil tidings; their hearts are firm,
secure in the Lord. Their hearts are steady, they will not be
afraid; in the end they will look in triumph on their foes.

—Psalm 112:7–8

*H*eavenly Father, I sometimes fear that the darkness is overcoming the light in our world and that all good things will be extinguished. At times like these, I need only to return to you, refreshing my faith in your holy Word. You are all-powerful, and righteousness will prevail. I trust in you, my Lord, and I know that I'm on the side of the Prince of Peace, who brings me comfort.

 *June 17*

We know that all things work together for good for those who love God, who are called according to his purpose.
—Romans 8:28

Quietly, calmly, Lord, you move in my life. Unseen yet always present, your love is a powerful force I can rely on when I feel alone and unsettled. Swiftly, surely, Lord, you work for my good. You always have my best interests in mind, and your timing is perfect in bringing goodness to my life. Strongly, securely I rest in your profound peace, a place I can always go to when I need to get away from the noise and the bustle. Sweetly, gently, you remind me each night when I lay down to sleep that you are watching over me and all is well in my world.

God's Spirit offers us the blessing of inner peace.

# June 18

Therefore, I tell you, her sins, which were many, have been forgiven; hence she has shown great love. But the one to whom little is forgiven, loves little.

—Luke 7:47

My great God, you have told us over and over in the Bible that to love is to forgive. Help me spread love to those around me through an unquestioning forgiveness of their transgressions, real and imagined. Help me stop "keeping score," and help me remember that we are to love endlessly, just as you love us. It is when I love others, Lord, that I bring your kingdom to this earth. Amen.

The power of true forgiveness cannot be overstated.

June 19

You will have confidence, because there is hope.
—Job 11:18

My God, send your Holy Spirit to whisper words of hope to me today. The gloomy clouds of discouragement seem to be closing in on me. I know this is temporary, but my hopes seem to be evaporating just now. Please renew me, Lord! Fill me with a new hope that's based not on what I see or feel but on what I know to be true of you and your love for me. Bless me with hope that's greater than any situation I face today, God. For I know my real hope is always in you.

Hope opens us to the new day coming.

June 20

You, Lord, have helped me and comforted me.
—Psalm 86:17

Almighty God, why is it we don't remember that you alone are the source of all comfort? Instead, when times are tough, we seek comfort in the things of the world that we see around us—in too much food, or drink, or late-night television. Those things can distract us, but we know they can never comfort us the way you do. Thank you for your faithfulness, Lord. For at the end of every one of our fruitless searches you are there, and in your presence we find true comfort.

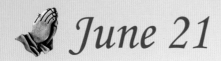 June 21

Now faith, hope, and love abide, these three;
and the greatest of these is love.
—1 Corinthians 13:13

*L*ove, hope, faith, and grace are just a few of the blessings you bring to me, Lord God. I pray that you may always see fit to cherish me as your child and continue to shower my life with the most amazing gifts of your Spirit. No material object can compare to the mercy you show, the forgiveness you offer, and the steadfast love and care you have for my family and me. I cherish these blessings as you cherish me, and I bow in gratitude each day. Thank you, dear God.

Lift up your heart in sweet surrender to the God
who is waiting to shower you with blessings.

June 22

Since there will never cease to be some in need on the earth,
I therefore command you, "Open your hand to the
poor and needy neighbor in your land."
—Deuteronomy 15:11

Father, I pray today for more compassion in the world. So many people feel uncared for and unloved. I ask that they be shown the same compassion that you have shown me. I pray that people take better care of each other and reach out to one another more, for this can be a cold, cold world. Help us all learn, Father, to be more giving and loving to each other and to take the time to take care of those who have no one to watch over them today. Amen.

God promises us his comfort, and he also uses
us as his agents to comfort others.

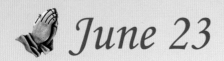# June 23

Those who wait for the Lord shall renew their strength, they shall mount up with wings like eagles, they shall run and not be weary, they shall walk and not faint.

—Isaiah 40:31

*L*ord, refresh my broken spirit tonight. Life has worn down the edges of my passion for living, and I am tired. Help me find a newfound sense of worth and wonder. Instill in me a sensation of seeing my life as if for the first time in all its magic. Renew in me the desire to be a light of good in the world and to fulfill the destiny you gave me upon the moment of my birth. Your Spirit is breath in my lungs and fire for my soul. Give me new wings upon which I can soar to the greatest of heights. Amen.

No matter how broken my life, God can create something new from the pieces.

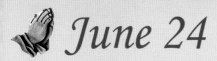

June 24

As having nothing, and yet possessing everything.
—2 Corinthians 6:10

$\mathcal{D}$ear Lord, it's tempting to look upon my life and feel overly proud for all that I have accomplished. But I know that everything I have has come from you, given freely to me because of your grace and not because of my actions. And so, I come to you now in humility, reminded of my weaknesses and sins and thankful for the abundance of gifts you have given me. Because of what Christ has done for me, I am yours—now and forever!

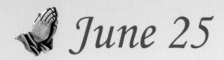

June 25

The Advocate, the Holy Spirit, whom the Father will
send in my name, will teach you everything, and
remind you of all that I have said to you.
—John 14:26

*H*eavenly Father, thank you for the centeredness you
bring to my life. Even when every external thing is in
an uproar, I can still come back to that still, small place
and feel your Holy Spirit. I know you are always with
me and that I am your beloved. I can rest in your
presence in complete peace, knowing you will protect
and shelter me. Thank you for your love, which never
fails. Amen.

Peace and tranquility are hidden
inside your own heart.

 # June 26

The God who has girded me with strength has opened my path. He made my feet like the feet of deer, and set me secure on the heights.

—2 Samuel 22:33–34

I thought my day couldn't get any worse, dear Lord, but you gave me a gift of hope for a better tomorrow. I thought things couldn't possibly be more of a mess, but you patiently waited for me to see that I could handle each and every mess with grace and dignity. I thought that I would always be alone, but you brought to me the love of good people, so they can live life alongside me. I thought my body couldn't bear any more labor, but you infused me with newfound strength. In you, Lord, I find hope and the promise of peace. Thank you, Lord.

If you do not hope, you will not find what is beyond your hopes.

—St. Clement of Alexandria

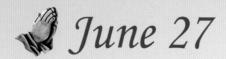# June 27

Come and see what God has done: he is awesome in his deeds
among mortals. He turned the sea into dry land;
they passed through the river on foot.
—Psalm 66:5–6

*I*n joy I celebrate my steadfast faith in you, heavenly

Father, and I know you have faith in me. You have

shown me your faith by trusting me with so many

lessons and challenges, and I have done my best to be

worthy of your faith. I celebrate the knowledge that

even when my world seems to be chaotic and crazy,

there is an unseen force of peace and love I can always

depend on to help me get through.

My faith is my foundation.

Thank you for the gift of faith.

 *June 28*

*I am the vine, you are the branches. Those who abide in me
and I in them bear much fruit, because apart
from me you can do nothing.*
—John 15:5

*A*lmighty God, no matter what I'm doing, I can
always tell if you are in it or not. When you are in it, my
tasks all seem to flow effortlessly. The plans I make fall
into place, and I can even see your hand in the details.
But when I've strayed from you and you're not a part
of my endeavors, well, that's when nothing seems to go
right. Teach me, God, that I need to bring my plans to
you before I commit to them. If you aren't involved, I
don't want to be, either. It's as simple and as profound
as that. Thank you for your willingness to be my partner in this, for together we can accomplish much.

 *June 29*

God is love, and those who abide in love abide in God, and God abides in them.

—1 John 4:16

*L*ord, it has been said that it is better to give than to receive, and in no case is this more true than in the ability to love others. My heart fills with joy when I can offer support, share my skills or knowledge, or simply just be with someone in pain. This ability to love others is a gift from you and is but a taste of what awaits us in heaven. Thank you for giving us a glimpse of your kingdom, and thank you for allowing me to become part of your good works on earth. Amen.

God loves us so that we can pass it on to others.

June 30

*Keep yourselves in the love of God; look forward to the mercy
of our Lord Jesus Christ that leads to eternal life.*

—Jude 21

$\mathcal{L}$ord, I come to you to pour my heart out to you
in gratitude for your many blessings. During the
Old Testament times, a father's greatest blessing was
bestowed on his first son. But you, in your goodness
and infinite generosity, have given all of your children
the same blessing—the gift of eternal life in Jesus
Christ. Thank you for sharing your greatest gift with
every one of us. You play no favorites, but you welcome
us all to your holy throne. Thank you for counting me
among your own.

*The object of our gratitude should
always be the Lord.*

My Prayer Life

_____

_____

_____

_____

_____

_____

_____

_____

_____

_____

_____

_____

_____

_____

_____

_____

_____

_____

_____

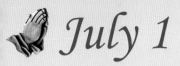

July 1

His master said to him, "Well done, good and trustworthy
slave; you have been trustworthy in a few things,
I will put you in charge of many things; enter
into the joy of your master."
—Matthew 25:23

$\mathcal{M}$y God, I fill my days with tasks and activities to give me status in the eyes of men and women, but I'm missing the most important fact: that because of your grace, nothing I can do can make you love me more or less. Meanwhile, help me seek your approval, not the approval of this fallen world. Let me take time from the "doing" to simply be with you, releasing myself and my life to your will more and more each day, dear Lord.

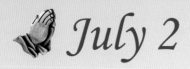

July 2

Now I am about to go the way of all the earth, and you know in your hearts and souls, all of you, that not one thing has failed of all the good things that the Lord your God promised concerning you; all have come to pass for you, not one of them has failed.

—Joshua 23:14

*G*od, my heart sings out today for all the good I have received. You have graced me with the love of so many wonderful people and prospered me in truly amazing ways. Each day I find new reasons to be grateful. Some are big and some are small, but all these things make me feel loved and cherished by you. Thank you for giving me a life that is truly fulfilling and for surrounding me with miracles big and small. Amen.

Thanksgiving is nothing if not a glad and reverent lifting of the heart to God in honour and praise for His goodness.

—James R. Miller

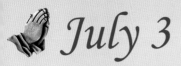 *July 3*

*O depth of the riches and wisdom and knowledge
of God! How unsearchable are his judgments
and how inscrutable his ways!*
—Romans 11:33

*D*ear heavenly Father, you are a god of paradox. You
brought your Son, our Savior, to us in the form of a
baby. You announced his coming first to the poorest
of shepherds. And you have told us that it is the weak
and humble, not the rich and proud, who will inherit
the earth. It is no surprise then that in order to have
everlasting life, we must first die. Just as Jesus died
on the cross and was raised to live again, we also will
receive eternal life after death. I pray that you will
remind me that much of what is true is beyond my
limited understanding. Help me trust in you and have
faith that with you even the impossible is possible.

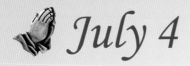 *July 4*

*D*ear God, you save us from so many terrible things, and yet I wonder if we stop often enough to recognize that your deliverance is one of the richest blessings you bestow. Today, Lord, I want to thank you for currently sparing this country from deadly plagues and violent wars on our own soil. All those things exist, we know full well, but today you are sparing us from them, and for that we are truly grateful. Amen.

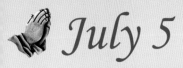

July 5

You have heard of this hope before in the word
of the truth, the gospel that has come to you.
—Colossians 1:5–6

$\mathcal{Y}$es, it feels good to have my hope back, heavenly
Father! I thought I had given up on life, but now I
realize there is so much more to look forward to and
that newfound hope is like a blazing light that fills the
dark corners of my heart. Hope has returned to me,
and I feel young, vital, and alive again, ready to take
on the world and grab opportunities by the horns. I'm
grateful, God, for this infusion of hope with which you
have filled my spirit.

When we live in hope, we cannot help
but notice all the ways in which
our lives are blessed.

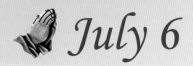 *July 6*

In him we have redemption through his blood, the forgiveness of our trespasses, according to the riches of his grace.

—Ephesians 1:7

*D*ear Jesus, you have given us the greatest gift imaginable through your birth and death—the gift of salvation. You have rescued us from despair and hopelessness by dying to atone for our sins. The forgiveness you have brought to our lives is the most precious gift we could ever hope for. Today, let me revel in the glory of redemption and know that I am saved, for this world and for all eternity. Amen.

The blessing of faith in the Lord is salvation.

July 7

While he was still far off, his father saw him and was
filled with compassion; he ran and put his
arms around him and kissed him.
—Luke 15:20

𝒟ear God, despite my best efforts and intentions, sometimes my path strays from yours. I fall into sin, and I'm ashamed of my weakness. But I come to you in faith and repentance, trusting that you will dust me off and open your arms wide, welcoming me back into your fold. I don't need to fear making mistakes, for you are a merciful and loving God, who longs to help me in my journey here on earth. Thank you for your continued love for me and for making me one of your children.

Faith lifts and supports,
filling spirits with assurance.

July 8

You shall not take vengeance or bear a grudge ... but you shall love your neighbor as yourself: I am the Lord.

—Leviticus 19:18

Lord, I can be so hardheaded. Once I assume a position, I dig in my heels and refuse to budge, just like Balaam's donkey in the Book of Numbers. Even when I'm sure of my position, I don't want to be stubborn and unyielding. Please help me be more compassionate to others and respectful of their opinions, especially when I think I'm right. Let me show my love and concern for them by listening honestly and openly to their thoughts and reasoning. I know this will make me a better friend and a better Christian.

God wants us to always treat others with the utmost care and respect.

 *July 9*

The Lord is near to all who call on him, to all who call on him in truth. He fulfills the desire of all who fear him; he also hears their cry, and saves them.
—Psalm 145:18–19

*L*ord, is peace possible when my life is filled with activities, responsibilities, and worries? I wish I had time to sit and just be with you— listening for your quiet voice amidst the tumult. Instead, I am caught up in the everyday, and I fear I'm moving farther from you. Please show me the way back to you, to your Word and your will for me. I know that the only way to find you is to seek you and that you will always find me.

The key to letting peace in is to invite God into every area of our life.

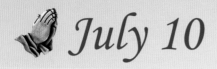# July 10

*No testing has overtaken you that is not common to everyone.
God is faithful, and he will not let you be tested beyond your
strength, but with the testing he will also provide the
way out so that you may be able to endure it.*

—1 Corinthians 10:13

God, I take comfort in the knowledge that you will never give me more than I can handle. I do ask you, though, to give me the strength and courage to handle what you've given me. I am grateful to be alive, but I could use some help right now in dealing with these feelings of anxiety and doubt. Give me the promise of your everlasting comfort so I may take that with me no matter what dark or stressful path life takes me down. You will be the lamp that guides my steps and warms my heart. Amen.

*God walks by your side every day
in every place.*

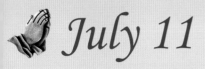

July 11

I will pour out my spirit on all flesh; your sons and your daughters shall prophesy, your old men shall dream dreams, and your young men shall see visions.

—Joel 2:28

Almighty God, only you could be creative enough to instill different passions in each of us. We love music, teaching, traveling, writing, singing—any number of pursuits—because you created us to be drawn to them. How empty life would seem without our passions! Don't let me neglect the passions you've given me, Lord, and most importantly, show me ways to pursue them to your glory. Thank you, Lord, for filling our hearts with passion for the things we love.

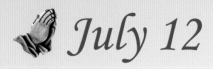 *July 12*

*Inquire of God that we may know whether
the mission we are undertaking will succeed.*
—Judges 18:5

*D*ear God, I badly need some advice. Things seem to be falling apart all around me, and I desperately want to make things better. My solutions, however, are not always the right ones for all those involved. Help me see things from all sides and all perspectives so that I'm guided to the best solution that will satisfy all involved. I ask for your wisdom today and the courage and fortitude to carry out your will no matter how difficult it might be or how much resistance I might face. Thank you, God, for being with me today as I try to resolve this problem.

July 13

Now may the Lord of peace himself give you peace at all times in all ways. The Lord be with all of you.
—2 Thessalonians 3:16

I celebrate today the peace that's from you and that's with me through all my days and never lets me down. God, your peace is my cornerstone, upon which I build the foundation of my life. In your peace, I spread peace to my family and friends, and to my community, for this indeed is a world that needs more peace. Blessed am I to have found that peace in you, God.

Great are the blessings of those who have peace in Christ.

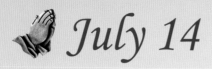 # July 14

> *Immediately the father of the child cried out,*
> *"I believe; help my unbelief!"*
> —Mark 9:24

*L*ord, how difficult it is for us to pray, believing that you hear us, but how necessary it is to do so—to express our gratitude in advance for all the answers you are preparing to lavish upon us as we pray. Help my unbelief, Lord. When I come to you in prayer, may I do so believing that you always have my best interests at heart. Whether your answer is yes, no, or not now, you do hear me! And so, Lord, I thank you even before I see evidence of your work in my life.

Faith is trusting in something that you can neither see nor touch, yet knowing it is always there guiding you along life's path.

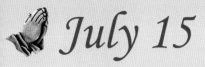 *July 15*

*They shall stand every morning, thanking and praising
the Lord, and likewise at evening.*
—1 Chronicles 23:30

The gentle flower does not give up when its sprouting
stem meets with the hardness of earth. No, it finds
hope within and pushes upward, bursting through the
ground and up into the light of the nurturing sun. It
drinks of the warmth and relishes the breeze, while
facing outward and never looking downward at the
earth again and lamenting where it came from. Let my
heart flower with the hope that never looks back and
never looks down. Thanks be to you, God almighty.

*Embrace the hope of each new morning and
the last ray of sunshine to fall at day's end.*

July 16

Be glad and rejoice, for the Lord has done great things!
—Joel 2:21

*H*ow abundant is your love, God! Indeed, your love appears in my life in the form of the wonderful people who walk through life with me. Moreover, you have blessed me with both material and immaterial treasures. I am deeply grateful for each blessing you give me, no matter where they come from or how big or small they are. Each day I look around me and I am reminded that the kingdom of heaven is truly spread out before me. Thank you, God.

Our spirits well up with the joy of Christ's love.

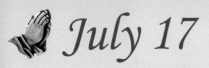

July 17

The Lord was not in the fire; and after the fire a sound of
sheer silence . . . Then there came a voice to him.
—1 Kings 19:12–13

*D*ear Lord and Father of mankind,

Forgive our foolish ways;

Reclothe us in our rightful mind,

In purer lives Thy service find,

In deeper reverence, praise.

Drop Thy still dews of quietness,

Till all our strivings cease;

Take from our souls the strain and stress,

And let our ordered lives confess

The beauty of Thy peace.

Breathe through the heats of our desire

Thy coolness and Thy balm;

Let sense be dumb, let flesh retire;

Speak through the earthquake, wind, and fire,

O still, small voice of calm.

—John Greenleaf Whittier

# July 18

The Lord's servant must not be quarrelsome but kindly to everyone, an apt teacher, patient, correcting opposition with gentleness.

—2 Timothy 2:24–25

Guide and encourage us, dear Lord, when we share the truths you have taught us. Often people are either angry or indifferent to what you have revealed in your holy Word, and when we try to express the good news about Jesus, they argue or ignore us. It is so easy to become impatient and angry ourselves. It is then that we need an extra measure of your Spirit to guide us in what we say and how we act in response. Please fill us with the love you have for these people so that we may be worthy ambassadors of Christ. Amen.

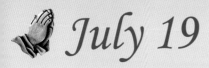# July 19

The Lord exists forever; your word is firmly fixed in heaven.
Your faithfulness endures to all generations.

—Psalm 119:89–90

*H*oly One, I have striven to do what is right in your eyes. I have followed your Word and obeyed your laws to the best of my ability. I now ask that you will be with me and comfort me. My needs are great and my power is small, but in you all things are possible. Please remove my burdens from me, for they are too heavy to carry without your help. Soothe me, love me, and care for me. I ask as your child. Amen.

You need not cry very loud:
he is nearer to us than we think.

—Brother Lawrence

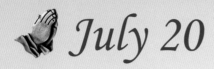 # July 20

Blessed are those who have not seen
and yet have come to believe.
—John 20:29

My Lord, what a joy it was to be able to visit the Holy Land and walk in places you walked! How inspiring to gaze out on the Sea of Galilee where you calmed the storm and to see the hillside where thousands gathered around to hear you teach the beatitudes! We never saw you, Lord, but we saw where you lived. Yet as meaningful as that experience was, we believed even before we journeyed there, for we see you everywhere in the faces of all those who believe in you and put their faith in you. Thank you, Lord, that we don't have to travel to the Holy Land to believe. We just have to open the doors to our hearts and welcome you in.

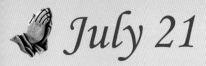 # July 21

Grace be with all who have an undying love
for our Lord Jesus Christ.
—Ephesians 6:24

Your grace, dear God, be upon me and those I love today. I know that many challenges are ahead, and I treasure the small ways you remind me that you are here to help guide me to make the right choices. I ask that you continue to fill my life with signs of your mercy and your love in those small whispers in my heart that tell me that I'm fulfilling your will. May your grace act as the lighthouse beacon that guides me to the shore, no matter how dark the night or how thick the fog before me. Amen.

I know I only have to call on him for
encouragement, direction, and guidance
to receive his loving assistance.

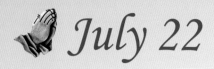 *July 22*

*Make haste, my beloved, and be like a gazelle
or a young stag upon the mountain of spices!*
—Song of Solomon 8:14

Dear Lord, my heart is feeling empty today, and I long for a true love to come into my life. Help me become the kind of person I look for in another, a partner and companion that will walk with me through life. Send me a love I can trust and believe in, who will stand up for me when the world threatens to push me down. I believe that you have created someone special just for me, so please prepare me to receive that special person, that we may be together soon.

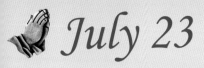 *July 23*

Let the little children come to me, and do not stop them; for it is to such as these that the kingdom of heaven belongs.
—Matthew 19:14

O Lord, how our hearts go out to the little children whose photographs we see with their big eyes, dirty faces, and bellies swollen from hunger. You know all the children in the world living in poverty, Lord. We sit at our comfortable kitchen tables and write checks to ministries who vow to help these children, but you know where all of them will lay their heads tonight, Lord. Be with them. In your great compassion, send them whatever it is they need to ease their suffering. We thank you so much for your great compassion.

An outstretched hand toward those in pain becomes a merciful extension of God's healing touch.

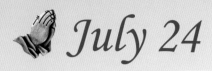 *July 24*

You were taught to put away your former way of life, your old self, corrupt and deluded by its lusts, and to be renewed in the spirit of your minds, and to clothe yourself with the new self, created according to the likeness of God in true righteousness and holiness.

—Ephesians 4:22–24

*L*ord, they say the definition of insanity is doing the same thing over and over again and expecting different results. I often find myself running around in circles, exhausted and resigned to my fate. But you alone have the power to show me new ways of thinking, of doing, and of being in the world. You alone can guide me to new paths I never imagined, where opportunities await and obstacles are few and far between. Each time I turn to you, I am reminded that every day is a new day and a new chance to live life in a whole new way. Amen.

From each of life's misfortunes comes a new beginning, an opportunity to renew your faith in the future.

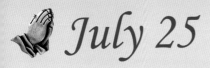

July 25

Rejoice and exult with all your heart.
—Zephaniah 3:14

*E*ach day brings new things to be happy about, God, and I am really loving my life for the first time in a long time. I am truly grateful for this new way of looking at things, seeing the glass half full instead of half empty and always looking on the bright side. Your blessings are everywhere, but it took me awhile to notice them because I was so caught up in the stress and strain of my daily life. Thank you for opening my eyes to a whole new world of wonder and joy.

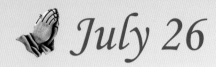

July 26

For I am convinced that neither death, nor life, nor angels,
nor rulers, nor things present, nor things to come, nor
powers, nor height, nor depth, nor anything else
in all creation, will be able to separate us from
the love of God in Christ Jesus our Lord.

—Romans 8:38–39

God, bring peace to the rough places in the world.
Bring hope to the hearts that have grown cold and love
to the souls that know only violence and despair. Bring
wisdom and understanding to those who see around
them only chaos. Bring comfort to those who suffer.
For you alone can show this world what true and lasting
peace is, the peace that is available to us all if we lay
down our prejudices and our pride and take up instead
the weapons of love and tolerance. God, bring peace
to the dark places of the world, that they may see your
light. Amen.

The wonder of God's peace is that even
when the world around us is in confusion,
underneath it all, we can know his peace.

 # July 27

You will seek the Lord your God, and you will find him if you
search after him with all your heart and soul.
—Deuteronomy 4:29

Dear Lord, sometimes I wonder if the things I say to
others lead them any closer to you at all. For example,
I use the word "hope" possibly too often: "Hope you
have a nice day!" "Hope you're feeling better soon!"
Help me put some substance to those hopes by turning
them into prayers. Remind me that earthly hopes
mean nothing without divine power and intervention.
Beginning today, Lord, I want to remember
to pray for those I encounter during
the day so that my hopes for them
have a much better chance of
connecting with your supreme will.

 *July 28*

*May the Lord direct your hearts to the love of God
and to the steadfastness of Christ.*
—2 Thessalonians 3:5

*H*eavenly Father, the joyfulness I feel inside I owe to you, for it reminds me that I'm loved and cared for no matter how many mistakes I make today or what I do wrong. I'm your child and will forever look up to you for guidance and direction, and I have faith that you will continue to show your everlasting love for me by providing me with just what I need when I need it. Because I have faith in your grace, I promise to always do my best, knowing that even if I fall short now and then, you will love me anyway.

To be loved is precious.

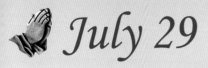 *July 29*

*I blessed the Most High, and praised and honored the
one who lives forever. For his sovereignty
is an everlasting sovereignty.*
—Daniel 4:34

Lord Jesus, the most real and lasting blessings are
those offered by you. The material things of this world
are transitory, and they will soon crumble to dust or
break and be worthless. But the gifts you have given us
are eternal. Please remind me today to seek after the
blessings of your kingdom, Lord, and
not of our world, so that I may
work toward that which is
everlasting and more valuable
than gold. I ask in your holy
name. Amen.

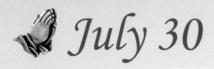# July 30

His lamp shone over my head, and by his light
I walked through darkness.

—Job 29:3

*G*od, the night before me is long and dark, and it is at times like this that I feel so lost and alone. Your love and presence is the manna I need to nourish my weary mind and strengthen my weakened spirit so that I can face the challenges of the morning. With you, God, I know that all is possible and that no matter how afraid I am, I never walk alone.

Be at peace with God, and he will
defeat the beast within.

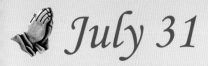 *July 31*

*Do not rejoice when your enemies fall, and do not let
your heart be glad when they stumble, or else
the Lord will see it and be displeased.*
—Proverbs 24:17–18

Heavenly Father, I come to you to ask that you help
me grow in compassion for others. It's easy to feel
concern for my family and friends and those I love.
It's simple to want the best for those whose daily lives
intersect with mine or for those whom I deem "innocent," such as children, victims of crimes, and the
poverty-stricken. It's much more difficult to expand my
circle of care to include those who have perpetrated
wrong against me personally or against society at large.
But you have commanded us to love everyone, not just
those we decide are deserving of our compassion.
Please remind me that all of us are your children and
all are deserving in your eyes. I ask in your awesome
name. Amen.

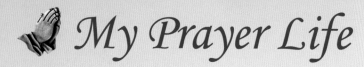

My Prayer Life

_____

_____

_____

_____

_____

_____

_____

_____

_____

_____

_____

_____

_____

_____

_____

_____

_____

_____

_____

_____

_____

August 1

The time is surely coming, says the Lord, when the one who plows shall overtake the one who reaps, and the treader of grapes the one who sows the seed; the mountains shall drip sweet wine, and all the hills shall flow with it.

—Amos 9:13

My Lord, please strengthen my faith so that nothing will disturb the calm waters in my heart. Make me a rock that does not move no matter how hard the waves crash up against it. During stormy days in my life, strengthen my faith so I will refuse to give up. Build my faith into a foundation that cannot be shaken so that I can be a rock to someone else today.

Faith makes the discords of the present the harmonies of the future.
—Robert Collyer

August 2

Do not let the sun go down on your anger,
and do not make room for the devil.
—Ephesians 4:26–27

Dear God, I have been hurt so many times by people, and I am tired of the pain and anger that is making my life miserable. Please help me find the power within to forgive those who have hurt me and to cut the ties that bind me to those bitter feelings and resentful emotions. I long to be free and at peace, and I know that the only path to peace is through forgiveness. Help me be the kind of person who is able to be honorable and noble by forgiving those who have hurt me. It is the hardest thing I have ever done, but with you, nothing is impossible.

One of the greatest peace-robbers
in our lives is anger.

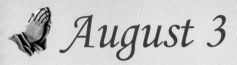# *August 3*

Listen, I will tell you a mystery! We will not all die, but we will all be changed, in a moment, in the twinkling of an eye, at the last trumpet. For the trumpet will sound, and the dead will be raised imperishable, and we will be changed.
—1 Corinthians 15:51–52

*L*ord, you sent your Son to us not to make our old lives better, but to give us entirely new lives in Christ. Help me cast off all my old ways of living and being so I can become something completely new and different. I don't just want to improve; I want to be reborn in Christ. I want to be like him. And so, I pray for the miracle of your love to change me, making me unrecognizable and completely, utterly yours. I ask in your name. Amen.

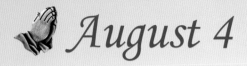

August 4

The spirit of the Lord God is upon me, ... to bind up the
brokenhearted, ... to comfort all who mourn.

—Isaiah 61:1–2

*H*eavenly Father, be with those who need you today.
So many in this world have never felt the peace that
passes understanding, the calm and serenity that
comes when we turn over our lives to your wise and
loving guidance. Instead, they live their lives alone, not
realizing you are only an arm's reach from them. For
each struggling soul, I pray that
you would offer them your
boundless mercy and
love, helping them come
to know you. Amen.

August 5

You shall love the Lord your God with all your heart, and with all your soul, and with all your mind, and with all your strength.

—Mark 12:30

My life is filled with love today, and I have you to thank, God, for bringing into my world a wonderful family and great friends. I could not have made better choices. I am surrounded by love and care, and I never feel alone in the presence of those you have permitted to walk alongside me on the path of life. And on those few occasions when I am alone, I know that your love, God, is ever present and infinite, and I am at peace in my heart.

We reflect the goodness of God most when we love others.

August 6

Make a joyful noise to the Lord, all the earth. Worship the Lord with gladness; come into his presence with singing. Know that the Lord is God. It is he that made us, and we are his; we are his people, and the sheep of his pasture.

—Psalm 100:1–3

*J*ust having your presence in my life, precious Jesus, is the greatest blessing of all. With you beside me, I know that all things are possible and I am never lacking in anything good. You have given me life and given it to me to live abundantly; I give thanks for the people, experiences, and things that you have chosen to bring into my life and for the lessons I have learned along the way. I don't need anything else but you, my Savior and Lord, for in you I already have everything.

The most important prayer in the world is just two words long: "Thank You."

—Meister Eckhart

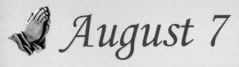

August 7

This Spirit he poured out on us richly through Jesus Christ our Savior, so that, having been justified by grace, we might become heirs according to the hope of eternal life.

—Titus 3:6–7

Heavenly Father, in our limited understanding of your generosity and of your abundant love for us, we sometimes act as if there were only a certain amount of grace to go around. We sort through our requests to determine which person is worthy of your grace or which situation should be blessed by your intervention. Forgive us for limiting you, Father. You are willing to lavish your grace upon us, and we don't want to turn away from all you want to give us. Thank you, Father, that your grace always overflows.

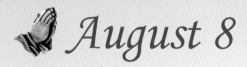

August 8

I prayed to the Lord my God and made confession, saying,
"Ah, Lord, great and awesome God, keeping covenant
and steadfast love with those who love you
and keep your commandments."

—Daniel 9:4

God, I sometimes forget to thank you for the things you have given me. I rush about my days and nights, distracted by the busyness, and forget to stop and look around at all the miracles you have brought into my life. Thank you. I mean that from the bottom of my heart. Thank you. I am overwhelmed by the mercy you have shown me when I screwed up, the grace you have given me when I most needed it, and the love you always give me, even when I don't act like I deserve it. Thank you so much, God.

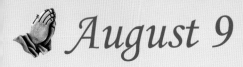

August 9

For I will restore health to you, and your wounds
I will heal, says the Lord.
—Jeremiah 30:17

God, when I could not walk another step, you lifted me up and we flew. When I could not get out of bed with illness, you restored me to health again. When I could not see the light at the end of the tunnel, you walked with me in the darkness until it appeared. When I could not find the solution to my problems, you filled my mind with fresh ideas and new ways of looking at things. To you I give thanks for always reviving my body, mind, and spirit when I feel I have nothing left to give. You are my rock and my sunlight, a place upon which to stand strong and a light to guide my way when I am ready to move forward again. Thank you, dear God.

Use stumbling blocks as stepping-stones to
move closer to the good in life.

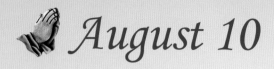 # August 10

Through him you have come to trust in God, who raised him
from the dead and gave him glory, so that your
faith and hope are set on God.

—1 Peter 1:21

I know of love, and I have faith in you, God, but even
so, I look around and sometimes lose hope at the state
of things in the world. There is so much violence and
misery, and the news is filled with sadness and despair.
I pray that you will show me the good in life, the good
we don't see on the nightly news, so that my hope will
again take root and flourish. Let me find hope again,
and then let me help others find their hope again, too.
This world needs all the hope it can get. Let me do my
part to spread the seeds of hope and watch that hope
blossom.

Hope is a gift that grows larger
when you give it away.

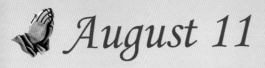

August 11

We look not at what can be seen but at what cannot be seen; for what can be seen is temporary, but what cannot be seen is eternal.

—2 Corinthians 4:18

O Lord, how my heart goes out to those who are in the midst of losing a loved one without the blessed assurance of eternal life! It can be terribly painful to watch someone we love fading away before our eyes. But because of faith in you, O Lord, we know this is not the only life we live. There is so much more to come—an eternity, in fact. Thank you, Lord, for the guarantee of eternal life for those who place their trust in you. It's not only a blessing to us when we die, but it also gives us hope when we lose those we love and who love you, for you are welcoming them into your heavenly kingdom.

For as long as God is beside us, nothing can take what is truly important from us.

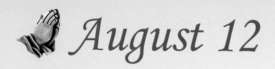

August 12

For God alone my soul waits in silence, for my hope is from him. He alone is my rock and salvation, my fortress; I shall not be shaken. On God rests my deliverance and my honor; my mighty rock, my refuge is in God.

—Psalm 62:5–7

*G*od, where do I turn when my life seems to be in a state of total upheaval? When family and job and health are all askew and nothing seems to be working out right? Please comfort me just as a parent comforts a child, rock me in your loving arms and whisper that it will all be better tomorrow. In your heavenly grace I will find the rest I need to face the new day with the wherewithal to handle anything set before me. Your comfort is the soothing balm I need right now to ease my worry and my fears. Thank you, God.

August 13

I regard everything as loss because of the surpassing
value of knowing Christ Jesus my Lord.
—Philippians 3:8

*L*ord Jesus, with your love and sympathy you have
granted us freedom from the bonds of self-hatred and
unending recrimination. We no longer have to be
chained to our pasts, destined to carry the weight of
our sins with us for all eternity. You felt our sadness
and hopelessness, and out of love, you assumed those
burdens yourself. Your compassion gave us absolution.
Thank you for your mercy and for the gift we can
never repay. Amen.

In God's grace, failure is never final but an
opportunity to learn and grow.

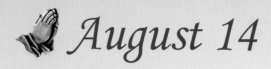 *August 14*

> *He himself bore our sins in his body on the cross, so that,*
> *free from sins, we might live for righteousness;*
> *by his wounds you have been healed.*
>
> —1 Peter 2:24

*M*y loving God, thank you for your mercy. I have sinned over and over, and still you open your arms and welcome me to you. I continue to try to keep true to your laws, but I also continue to fail time and time again. The only thing that gives me the courage to stand up and try again is the knowledge that you will always love me and will always forgive me as long as I try to faithfully live according to your laws. Thank you for your loving presence in my life.

The blessing of God's forgiveness is
that he heals our wounds.

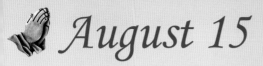

August 15

I want their hearts to be encouraged and united in love, so that they may have all the riches of assured understanding and have the knowledge of God's mystery, that is, Christ himself, in whom are hidden all the treasures of wisdom and knowledge.

—Colossians 2:2–3

*A*lmighty God, the Giver of Wisdom, without whose help resolutions are vain, without whose blessing study is ineffectual, enable me, if it be Thy will, to attain such knowledge as may qualify me to direct the doubtful and instruct the ignorant, to prevent wrongs, and terminate contentions; and grant that I may use that knowledge which I shall attain to Thy glory and my own salvation.

—Samuel Johnson, "Almighty God, the Giver of Wisdom"

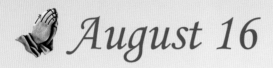

August 16

*Keep on doing the things that you have learned
and received and heard and seen in me,
and the God of peace will be with you.*
—Philippians 4:9

O Lord, sometimes I wonder if you look down on me during the day and just shake your head at how scattered I am. As I'm pulled in one direction after the next, my life must look anything but peaceful to you. I confess that I sometimes lose the inner peace you graciously granted me when I first believed. Restore that peace in my heart, Lord, and let others see in my life the peace that could only have come from you.

*We can achieve inner peace by acknowledging
our turmoil, then shifting our focus
toward the healing we desire.*

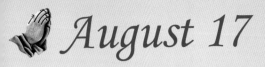 # *August 17*

*Create in me a clean heart, O God, and put
a new and right spirit within me.*
—Psalm 51:10

*L*ord, I know you created me and you don't make mistakes, but sometimes I think I need an extreme makeover. I'm not talking about the outward me this time, I'm talking about the inner me, the me that only I know. My heart, my attitudes, my feelings, even my thoughts about my family could use some refreshing, Lord. I give you permission to do some serious remodeling in this house called me. I trust you and only you to make me over, knowing you will also make me completely perfect someday.

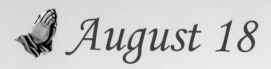

August 18

The Almighty... will bless you with blessings of heaven above.
—Genesis 49:25

*F*ather in heaven, when I count my blessings, I am overwhelmed with the sheer number of gifts you have given me. My friends, my family, the world around me, the air I breathe, and the bed in which I lay my head each night—all these things are testaments to your greatness and generosity. Please let me continue to daily count my blessings so that I may always be reminded of how much you love me, and how good you are.

# August 19

Keep alert, stand firm in your faith, be courageous, be strong.
Let all that you do be done in love.
—1 Corinthians 16:13–14

*D*ear Lord, I think I'm doing a pretty good job on
your commandment to love my neighbors. But loving
my enemies—I'm stuck. I'm having so much trouble
loving those I disagree with or dislike, or those who
hurt me or who have done me wrong. Please help me
see my way to dealing with them with compassion and
love, despite my earthly emotions. If I can see them
and their actions through your eyes, I will be able
to treat them as cherished children of God who are,
themselves, hurting and in need of love. That is such
a tough order, and I can only do it with your help.

Loving our enemies proves that we belong
to God, for he loves everyone, no
matter what they have done.

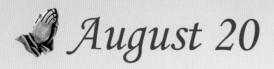

August 20

Restore us to yourself, O Lord, that we may be restored;
renew our days as of old.
—Lamentations 5:21

*G*od, I feel terribly lost. I'm stuck in this dark place of sadness and hopelessness, and my faith is nowhere to be found. I ask in prayer for your loving assistance— that you may return to me the faith that can move mountains and overcome any obstacle. I have many obstacles to overcome, and I have no idea how to do it. Please help me find that faith that reminds me that I'm never alone, that you can get me through this, and that I will be the better for it.

The more we seek the light,
the brighter it becomes.

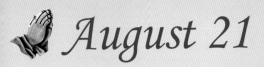

August 21

*"Look, the virgin shall conceive and bear a son, and they
shall name him Emmanuel," which means, "God is with us."*

—Matthew 1:23

*D*ear Lord, when I fall on my knees
out of despair and feel that I'm alone
in the world, that is when I sense your
presence most clearly. Through my tears,
I feel your love for me, gentle and reassuring,
letting me know that there is hope in the midst of
pain. Thank you for never forsaking me, but for
finding me wherever I am. I
would be utterly lost in the
most desperate sense
without you.

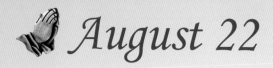

August 22

For where your treasure is, there your heart will be also.

—Luke 12:34

*T*each me, Lord, to look at the world with hope and expectation, not with despair and cynicism. I am grateful for all you have done for me, but there is still this emptiness inside that catches up to me now and then. Help me see how wonderful my life is, just as it is, and that nothing more is needed for me to be happy and at peace, for those are gifts that come from you. Teach me to keep my eyes on the bounty that comes from a thankful heart, not from the things we acquire but from the experiences we have and the love we give. Amen.

*If we can cherish just one precious gift,
our lives will be rich indeed.*

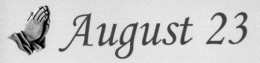 *August 23*

> *Happy are those whose transgression is forgiven,*
> *whose sin is covered.*
>
> —Psalm 32:1

*M*y Lord, this world continues to have an obsession with whatever can make us happy. Ads proclaim that we can't be happy without this product or that service, and so we add to the long list of things that may please us for a while, but can't deliver true happiness. Forgive our fruitless chasing after happiness, Lord, for we know that it can only exist in relationship with you. Until we know you and seek your forgiveness, we really can't know happiness. But with you, we are full of joy!

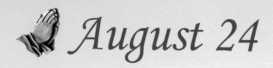# August 24

So then you are no longer strangers and aliens, but you are citizens with the saints and also members of the household of God, built upon the foundation of the apostles and prophets, with Christ Jesus himself as the cornerstone.

—Ephesians 2:19–20

My Lord, it is in you that we live and move and have our being. You not only hold the direction of our lives in your hands, but you also control every breath we take. By your will we have the gift of this day to live and work and love under your watchful eye. Let us never forget that you are the one in charge, Lord. Keep us ever mindful of your compassion for us, and keep us ever attentive to your guidance in our lives.

God helps me build a firm foundation by showing me how to rely on his wisdom, seek his direction, and walk in his path.

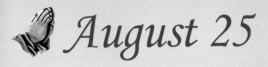

August 25

He will feed his flock like a shepherd; he will gather the lambs in his arms, and carry them in his bosom, and gently lead the mother sheep.

—Isaiah 40:11

Comfort me, O God, as I seek shelter from the storms of everyday life. I am grateful for the good things I have, but sometimes I feel I cannot carry the burden of life's challenges alone. Remind me with your loving presence that no matter what my day brings me, you are there for me, with me—and on my behalf— making smooth the way before me. In your love, I find true rest. Amen.

We find a resting place in God's enduring love, and we know that his plan for us is good.

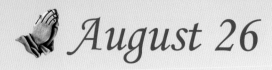

August 26

The Lord, a God merciful and gracious, slow to anger, and abounding in steadfast love and faithfulness.

—Exodus 34:6

What a gift mornings are in our lives, Lord! When the sun begins to rise over the plains, casting its pink light across the face of the mountains, we forget all about yesterday's challenges and failures. The new day, when we turn it over to you in prayer, is full of joyful anticipation. Thank you, Lord, for giving us a brand new start each morning as we wake. Your eternal mercy blesses us day by day.

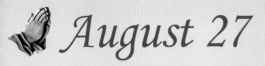

August 27

Every generous act of giving, with every perfect gift, is from above, coming down from the Father of lights.

—James 1:17

*H*eavenly Father, when we sit down to eat, we say "grace" before our meal. Through this simple act we ask for your blessing upon our food, and we also thank you for the marvelous gifts we have received from you. Each time I encounter a gift in my life, remind me to greet it in the same way, first asking your blessing and then expressing my thanks. Truly all good things come from you, Father.

All simple pleasures are opportunities for grateful praise.

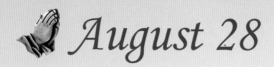# August 28

As a deer longs for flowing streams,
so my soul longs for you, O God.
—Psalm 42:1

*S*o many times in my life, Lord, I have felt my faith drain out of me, leaving me feeling high and dry. Lost and afraid, I have wandered alone and felt the abandonment of those I thought were my friends. I pray that you will never abandon me and that you will strengthen my faith again so that I will never feel horribly alone. I know that you are always with me, but my heart and my soul need to be reminded of that daily, especially when things get chaotic and I feel as if I am at the end of my rope. Please give me the faith I need to get through one day at a time, for I know that will be enough.

Great faith is not found; it is made of tiny
demonstrations of commitment
on a daily basis.

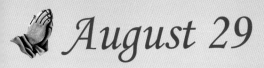 *August 29*

*To those who are called, who are beloved in God the Father
and kept safe for Jesus Christ: May mercy, peace,
and love be yours in abundance.*

—Jude 1–2

*L*ord, how often in our search for peace do we forget to simply follow your gentle guidelines? You tell us to forgive others. If we do, we will have peace. You tell us to love our enemies. If we do, we will have peace. You tell us not to worry about what we will wear or what we will eat, but to take comfort by considering the lilies of the field and the birds in the air. If we do, we will have peace. You tell us not to worry so much about storing up stuff, but to store up treasures in heaven. If we do, we will have peace. Thank you, Lord, for showing us the way. Keep our feet on the path to peace that you planned for us. Amen.

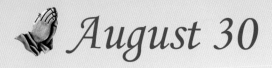

August 30

*All these blessings shall come upon you and overtake you, if
you obey the Lord your God: Blessed shall you be when you
come in, and blessed shall you be when you go out.*
—Deuteronomy 28:2, 6

God, I thank you today for the many blessings that fill
my life with little joys and big miracles. I'm in awe that
you have seen fit to shower your kindness upon me
and my loved ones, and never for a moment do I take
for granted what you have done for me. I live each day
in thankfulness and appreciation, even for the challenges you put before me, knowing that many blessings
come to me in countless ways. Thank you, God, for
continuing to bless me as you do.

*When you focus on the good in your life,
it tends to attract even more.*

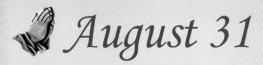

August 31

I will forgive their iniquity, and remember their sin no more.
—Jeremiah 31:34

$\mathcal{D}$ear Lord, I wish I had your ability to forget sin. How marvelous that you promise to remove our sin as far as the east is from the west and to remember it no more! Every time we confess a sin to you, it's as if it's the first time we've sinned. Lord, I'm just not good at forgetting sins, even if I can forgive them. It's my nature to hold onto grudges and to remember everything from the unintentional slight to the egregious sin. Help me, Lord! Give me your amazing ability to forgive—and forget.

My Prayer Life

_____

_____

_____

_____

_____

_____

_____

_____

_____

_____

_____

_____

_____

_____

_____

_____

_____

_____

_____

September 1

[Jesus taught,] "You shall love your neighbor as yourself."
—Mark 12:31

God, I thank you for the blessing of love from good friends. My friends shower me with love and care every day, and I feel comfort knowing they are always there for me. I am so grateful for each one of them, as different and unique as they are, and for the things they teach me. My friends are like gemstones, so priceless and beautiful. Thank you for friends old, for friends new, and for friends yet to come.

What a blessing to have someone who wants to share all our joys and sorrows!

September 2

I am like an evergreen cypress;
your faithfulness comes from me.
—Hosea 14:8

*D*ear God, the ability to talk to
you directly and bring my cares
and needs to you is nothing short
of incredible. That a being of your
magnitude and limitless power wants
to have a personal relationship with each of your
creatures amazes me. Thank you for giving us the
opportunity to feel your presence daily. Knowing you
are near me makes me love you more.

Our delight in God's love cannot compare
with his joy in loving us.

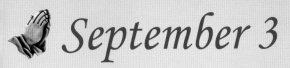

September 3

I have been crucified with Christ; and it is no longer I who live, but it is Christ who lives in me.
—Galatians 2:19–20

*D*ear Jesus, with your death, you gave me hope. I no longer have to fear the future or shy away from death. Lord, you have liberated me through your selfless sacrifice. I accept your gift with open arms, embracing you and the life you have promised me. Thank you for giving yourself wholly for me, and I endeavor to do the same—to offer my life to you and to your will. Take me and use me, for I am yours. Amen.

September 4

For you, O Lord, have blessed and are blessed forever.
—1 Chronicles 17:27

Almighty God, I thank you for giving me the ability to be blessed by simple things. A friend drives by as I'm walking, and my mood is lightened by her smile and her wave. Three deer stroll across my lawn and peek in at my office window. A hummingbird lingers over me just a moment while I'm reading outdoors as if to say hello. My life is tremendously rich with simple moments like these, Lord. I recognize that each and every one is a blessing from you, and I thank you.

Take the time to slow down and count your blessings.

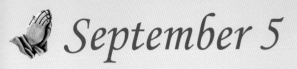# September 5

Like obedient children, do not be conformed to the desires that you formerly had in ignorance. Instead, as he who called you is holy, be holy yourselves in all your conduct; for it is written, "You shall be holy, for I am holy."
—1 Peter 1:14–16

Lord, in you I find renewal and the courage to see life in a different way. By following your will, I am filled with an excitement, energy, and enthusiasm for life that recharges my purpose and gives me new hope that all will be well. I thank you for this chance to do things differently, with a different perspective, and to follow the light you shine for me, making my path easier. In your presence I know I can accomplish anything and live my dreams. Amen.

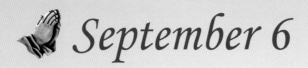

September 6

They shall obtain joy and gladness, and sorrow and sighing shall flee away. I, I am he who comforts you.

—Isaiah 51:11–12

Lord, why is it that when the struggles, challenges, and hurts of life press in upon me, even my physical presence is downtrodden? In times of trial and grief I sometimes feel as if I'm just struggling through quicksand with my head bowed and my eyes downcast. But you, O Lord, are the lifter of my head. In time, I realize that looking down won't solve anything but looking up will. I praise you, Lord!

Trust in the comfort of the Lord.

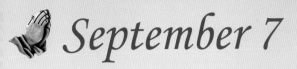

September 7

*He shall stand and feed his flock in the strength of the Lord,
in the majesty of the name of the Lord his God. And they
shall live secure, for now he shall be great to the ends
of the earth; and he shall be the one of peace.*

—Micah 5:4–5

God grant me a peace that is steadfast
and true, a peace that never fails me
no matter what is going on in my
world. Give to me a soft place to
fall and a shelter in which my heart
and soul can stay dry from the rain.
Your peace gives me hope, faith, and strength and
allows me to be strong for others who may need me.
Make me an instrument of your
peace so that even as I help myself,
I can help everyone else around
me. Thank you, God.

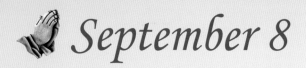 *September 8*

The grace of the Lord Jesus Christ be with your spirit.
—Philippians 4:23

*D*ear Lord, thank you for showing us through your
Word how your early followers cared for one another.
Whether in greeting or at a time of departure, they
often asked for a blessing of grace for one another. So
do we, Lord. Please send your blessing of grace to all
those we love, all those we encounter,
and all those we hope to lead
closer to you. And may your
grace encourage us and lift our
spirits, just as it did for all who
received it in centuries past.

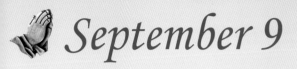

September 9

*We have not ceased praying for you and asking that you may
be filled with the knowledge of God's will in all spiritual
wisdom and understanding, so that you may lead lives worthy
of the Lord, fully pleasing to him, as you bear fruit in every
good work and as you grow in the knowledge of God.*

—Colossians 1:9–10

*F*ather in heaven, one of the biggest challenges we
face is our attempt to understand things through your
eyes. It simply can't be done fully here on earth, but
that shouldn't stop us from trying or even from asking
you why you do things the way you do. At the same
time please keep us humble, Father. We know that
your ways are not always our ways, but from your
eternal perspective they always lead us in the right
direction for our lives. Never give up on us. We need
your guidance in our lives, and we welcome it. Thank
you for your forgiveness when we question you instead
of simply trusting you.

*The loving Spirit that created you is always
available to guide you into a better life.*

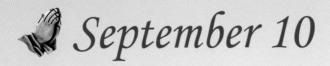 # *September 10*

Each of you must give as you have made up your mind,
not relunctantly or under compulsion,
for God loves a cheerful giver.
—2 Corinthians 9:7

Lord, sometimes I'm overwhelmed with all the opportunities for showing compassion through monetary giving. We're deluged with requests in the mail, over the phone, and on the streets. We want to be generous with what you've given us, Lord, but I don't believe you expect us to honor all these requests. Please give us your wisdom and lead us, so that we can discern which requests are ours to fulfill and which ones will be met by others. We want to be compassionate yet wise stewards of all we have been given, Lord. Everything we have comes from you, so please let us know how you want it distributed.

September 11

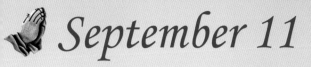

For the Lord will not reject for ever. Although he causes grief, he will have compassion according to the abundance of his steadfast love.
—Lamentations 3:31–32

$\mathcal{D}$ear Lord, whenever I face challenges to my faith, I wonder why you would allow me to be tested. I've already committed my life to you—isn't that enough? But then I realize that an untested faith is no faith at all and that it is necessary for me to go through difficult times in order to strengthen my resolve and my commitment to the Christian life. So now, I welcome these times. I know they will be tough, but I also know that with your help I will prevail over every temptation. Thank you for giving me these opportunities to grow in faith and to learn to rely on you more and more.

Faith forms the bedrock upon which I stand, unswayed despite the winds of change.

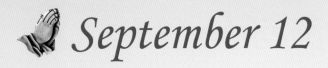

September 12

There is no distinction, since all have sinned and fall short of the glory of God; they are now justified by his grace as a gift, through the redemption that is in Christ Jesus.

—Romans 3:22–24

*S*overeign God, I have fallen short of your plan for me. I'm ashamed and disappointed. I have given in to temptation and let my weakness get the best of me. Now I stand before you, asking once again for your forgiveness and grace. Because of the promises you made to me, I know you won't keep your blessings from me. Thank you for being a merciful God, withholding no good thing from me. Amen.

To receive grace means that we are given good things in this life whether we deserve them or not.

September 13

Those of steadfast mind you keep in peace—in peace because they trust in you. Trust in the Lord forever, for in the Lord God you have an everlasting rock.
—Isaiah 26:3–4

*H*eavenly Father, let me carry your peace inside me today and use it as an anchor against the tumult of my daily life. It's so easy to get lost in my routines and my to-do list. The day's demands threaten to blow me off-course, but the knowledge of your strength and omnipotence can serve as a touch point, bringing me back to serenity again and again. Help me remember that peace is only a heartbeat away, whatever my outward circumstances.

The blessing of peace grows best in the soil of faith and wisdom.

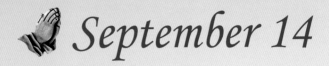 # *September 14*

*If then your whole body is full of light, with no part of it
in darkness, it will be as full of light as when
a lamp gives you light with its rays.*

—Luke 11:36

Let me be a light in the dark, Lord. Use me to my
fullest capabilities as a force for compassionate good in
the world. There is so much to be sad and depressed
about and so many people crying out in need. Help
me know the best way to serve the world—to reach out
to those people and help to dry their tears. Let me be
your light in the dark, dear Lord, shining
like a beacon so that all who are lost can
follow you. Amen.

*Today is the day to reach out
and lend a helping hand.*

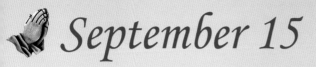

September 15

Listen! I am standing at the door, knocking; if you hear
my voice and open the door, I will come in to you
and eat with you, and you with me.
—Revelation 3:20

I came to you late, O Beauty so ancient and new.
I came to love you late. You were within me and I
was outside where I rushed about wildly searching for
you like some monster loose in your beautiful world.
You were with me but I was not with you. You called
me, you shouted to me, you wrapped me in your
Splendour, you broke past my deafness, you bathed me
in your Light, you sent my blindness reeling. You gave
out such a delightful fragrance and I drew it in and
came breathing hard after you. I tasted, and it made
me hunger and thirst; you touched me, and I burned
to know your Peace.

—Saint Augustine of Hippo

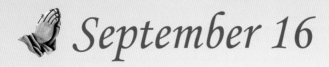 *September 16*

Who is a God like you, pardoning iniquity...? He does not retain his anger forever, because he delights in showing clemency. He will again have compassion upon us; he will tread our iniquities under foot. You will cast all our sins into the depths of the sea.

—Micah 7:18–19

*L*ord, you forgive us all our transgressions, and for that I am grateful. Though I strive to always do the right thing, I know that my sins will be forgiven if they are made with a heart willing to learn and to grow. By forgiving me, you free me to be who I am, warts and all, always knowing that I am loved no matter how badly I behave. I aspire to be perfect in your eyes, Lord, but it is good to know that if I fall short now and then, all is forgiven.

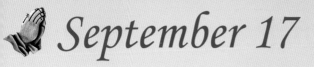

September 17

Do not fear, greatly beloved, you are safe.
Be strong and courageous!
—Daniel 10:19

*B*arren is my heart tonight, Lord. I've been hurt and broken, and I feel as though I can't go on. Worse still, I feel there is no point. I pray that you watch over me as I lay down to rest. While I sleep, fill me with hope and faith, just enough to get through one more day. For I know that if I can make it through one day, you will empower me again to make it through another. I pray that your strength will be mine and your courage will inspire me to face my problems with a renewed belief that with you at my side, I will come out stronger and better than ever. Come walk with me through this barren plain, and guide me to the valley of blessings that awaits over the horizon, just out of sight.

Tell God how you feel because if you voice your
pain, it can be whisked away in the wind.

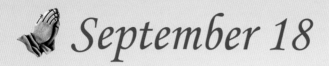# *September 18*

Be strong and bold; have no fear or dread of them,
because it is the Lord your God who goes with
you; he will not fail you or forsake you.
—Deuteronomy 31:6

*H*eavenly Father, thank you for being there when I needed you today. I was scared and confused, and I turned to you in prayer and asked for your guidance. You were immediately with me, surrounding me with your presence. The challenges I was facing didn't go away, but I was able to see them more clearly and realize they are less significant than I had feared. I am so grateful that you are always with me and always ready to help me in my times of need. Thank you for your love for me. Amen.

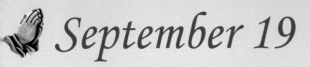 *September 19*

In all these things we are more than conquerors
through him who loved us.
—Romans 8:37

*D*ear Lord, I have been fighting these battles for so
long, and now I can see the glimmer of change on the
horizon. My faith has been rewarded and my energy is
renewed because your kingdom on earth is closer than
ever. I trust that everything is unfolding moment by
moment according to your holy plan. I just need to
stay the course until your time is at
hand. Thank you, Father, for
your goodness.

*There's a place of renewal and
happiness within you.*

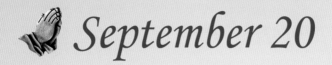# *September 20*

> *For in hope we were saved. Now hope that is seen is not hope. For who hopes for what is seen? But if we hope for what we do not see, we wait for it with patience.*
> —Romans 8:24–25

$\mathcal{D}$ear loving God, let all else be taken from me but my hope in you. My hope is what keeps me going even when all seems lost. My hope is my bond to you, and my faith in you is the food that nourishes me back to strength when I am weakened. Without hope, I have nothing, but with hope, I have every good thing. Hope, dear God, is your breath upon me—a breath that is warm and comforting and true. Hope is the song my heart continues to sing, even when the music has stopped all around me. Thank you for the hope you have given me.

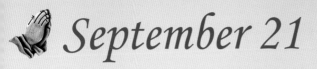

September 21

We are ambassadors for Christ, since God is making his appeal through us.
—2 Corinthians 5:20

*L*ord Jesus, others see the miracles you have done in my life, and they know the special relationship I have with you, my Savior. They are turning to me for guidance, but my earthly counsel is not enough. I need your wisdom as I provide advice and direction for them. Please use me as your mouthpiece so that only godly words may pass through my lips. Help me be a testament to your goodness.

If we pray for his assistance, God will help us reach out to our neighbor with his love.

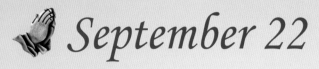

September 22

*Strive for his kingdom, and these things
will be given to you as well.*
—Luke 12:31

*L*ord, you said to first seek your kingdom and all else will be given me. I tried for so long to seek those other things first, those material things I thought would make me happy, and all it left me was feeling lost and alone and cold. But the kingdom you offer is one of love, mercy, and everlasting comfort. Your wisdom is far more precious than rubies and more priceless than gold. I understand that all good things can come to me only when I first immerse myself in your loving presence. That thought brings me a comfort nothing outside of me ever could. Thank you, God.

*Just a tiny seed of faith grows into a majestic
tree of blessings.*

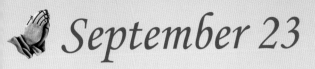# September 23

The patient in spirit are better than the proud in spirit.

—Ecclesiastes 7:8

*L*ord, help me be patient with my children, loving
with my spouse, and caring to my family even when
they tax and trouble me. Your compassion has given
me the strength to be a rock to those who depend on
me. I would like to have compassion for others, so that
I may be their rock in times of despair. Build in me
a character worthy of your love, and show me how to
give the fruits of that love to those in need. Amen.

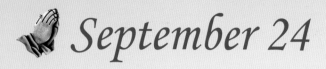

September 24

For you who revere my name the sun of righteousness shall rise, with healing in its wings. You shall go out leaping like calves from the stall.

—Malachi 4:2

*T*oday, dear God, I celebrate your awesome love in my life, and I want everyone to know about it. You have never let a day go by without showing me that you love me utterly and completely and that I walk in your grace and mercy at all times. I celebrate sharing your presence with everyone with whom I come into contact, spreading that heavenly grace to all I can so that they, too, can join in this celebration.

Only God's love can truly satisfy my soul.

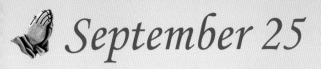

September 25

*The law of the Lord is perfect, reviving the soul; . . . the
commandment of the Lord is clear, enlightening the eyes. . . .
More to be desired are they than gold, even much fine gold;
sweeter also than honey, and drippings of the honeycomb.*
—Psalm 19:7–8, 10

*D*ear God, you have told us that if we humbly follow

your commandments, you will bless us. I have done the

best I can, striving to act in accordance with your laws.

But I still feel abandoned by you, and I feel lonely and

unloved. I know you are here with me, and my faith

continues to be strong, but why can't I hear you or feel

your loving touch? Please, I pray, send a sign that I

have not been forgotten by you. Let me see your love

for me so that I may joyfully do your will. And please

give me strength to continue on my path until you

show your face to me again. These things I ask in your

cherished name. Amen.

*God will never give us a burden to bear without
giving us the grace to endure it.*

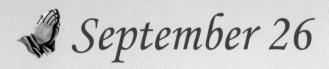

September 26

Set the believers an example in speech and conduct,
in love, in faith, in purity.
—1 Timothy 4:12

*L*ord, please help me serve as an example for others who are hoping to renew their lives. I want them to look at me and know of your transformative powers. I want to show them how you, heavenly Father, can take something dead and wasted in spirit and turn it into a living, thriving being, overflowing with love. You have worked miracles in my life, and I want to be a testament to your holy power. Mold me into your image, so I may encourage others in their journeys.

Love is at the heart of all healing.

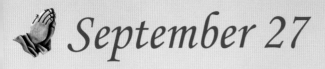

September 27

For I have no pleasure in the death of anyone,
says the Lord God. Turn, then, and live.
—Ezekiel 18:32

$\mathcal{D}$ear Lord, oftentimes when people say they hope for something, it sounds like a wish they know will never be granted. But because I am a Christian, what I hope for most—eternal life in Christ—will indeed come to pass one day. Please help me reach out to my friends and acquaintances who do not yet know you. Help me find the right words to tell them that knowing Jesus is the sweetest and best hope that anyone could ever have, all the better because it is possible, right now, today. Help me spread the word of your love for the world so that everyone has the opportunity to know you as I do.

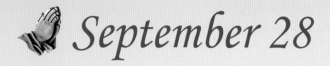# *September 28*

> *If there is among you anyone in need, a member of your community in any of your towns within the land that the Lord your God is giving you, do not be hard-hearted or tight-fisted toward your needy neighbor.*
>
> —Deuteronomy 15:7

*S*overeign Lord, as part of my spiritual journey here on earth, I want to grow in my ability to love and care for others. You have provided us such a wonderful example in your Son, Jesus Christ, and I ask that you help me follow in his path, giving with all my heart to everyone I encounter. Please continue to show me how to develop my ability to love others, knowing what to offer them and how to meet their needs. I ask in your name. Amen.

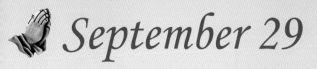

September 29

For from the rising of the sun to its setting my name is great among the nations, and in every place incense is offered to my name, and a pure offering; for my name is great among the nations, says the Lord of hosts.

—Malachi 1:11

*L*ike the low-lying fog that seeps over the mountains and blankets the countryside, grief seems to pervade every part of me each time it comes. I can't think clearly, see clearly, or move freely being encumbered by this fog. But you, O Lord, eventually send the sun. Slowly, gratefully, the fog begins to lift. And as it does, it leaves in its place your healing comfort...and the hope to go on. Thank you, Lord.

There be no potion so powerful as the certain belief that something good can happen tomorrow.

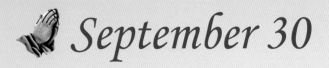

September 30

Be strong, be courageous, and keep the charge of the Lord
your God, walking in his ways . . . so that you may
prosper in all that you do and wherever you turn.
—1 Kings 2:2–3

How do I handle this situation, heavenly Father?
I have tried my ways, and my ways rarely work out
well. I know that your thoughts are far superior to my
thoughts and that your ways are far better than my
ways. And so, Lord, I pray for your guidance and the
will to carry out your directions. Let me be a channel
for your purpose and your will in this
situation, knowing that as I surrender my problems to you, they are
already resolved in the best way
possible. Amen.

Begin to weave and God will give the thread.
—German proverb

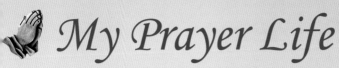

My Prayer Life

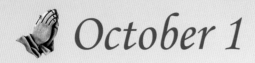 *October 1*

> *I said, "I will confess my transgressions to the Lord,"*
> *and you forgave the guilt of my sin.*
> —Psalm 32:5

*H*eavenly Father, I know I need you not only to forgive my sin but also to forgive the guilt I feel because of it. When I feel guilty, I keep dredging up my sins as if they weren't really forgiven. I'm truly sorry if that insults and offends you, Lord. You have told me again and again that I am forgiven. I thank you with my whole heart for not only forgiving me but also for taking away the guilt of my sin.

*Only when we are ready to relinquish
the hurt is there an opportunity for
forgiveness and healing to begin.*

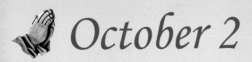

October 2

Give thanks to the Lord, for his steadfast love endures forever.
—2 Chronicles 20:21

Lord, I sat down with a big list of things to ask you
for. Material needs and wants, people to reach, hearts
to change, and situations where your presence is
needed. But as I began to pray, I realized how many
blessings I already have in my life and that I have more
than I could ever need. So I am setting aside my list
of petitions, and I want to say only this:
Thank you. Thank you for being a
loving and responsive God who
anticipates and answers my
needs. Amen.

# October 3

*Let the words of my mouth and the meditation of my heart
be acceptable to you, O Lord, my rock and my redeemer.*

—Psalm 19:14

O Lord Jesus, thank you for all the monuments to faith you have strategically placed in my life. Whenever I feel myself beginning to doubt that you will intervene in a given situation, all I have to do is look back and remember when you took care of me in the past. Crises with teenagers, the pain of financial reverses, and grieving the loss of friends and parents—I reflect on all those times and see how you faithfully worked to bring me safely through them and closer to you at the same time. Looking back increases my faith going forward, dear Lord. I praise you for the monuments of faith.

*With the power of faith we need not search for
answers outside of the Lord.*

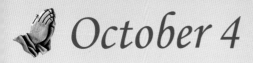# October 4

The Lord is my shepherd, I shall not want. He makes me lie
down in green pastures; he leads me beside still waters;
he restores my soul.

—Psalm 23:1–3

When I was a child, I had my favorite blanket. I took that blanket everywhere, wrapping myself in its warmth and comfort. Now I am all grown up, and you, God, are the one I turn to for that warmth and comfort. Like that blanket, I know all I have to do is call you, and you will wrap your love around me and make me feel safe and snug. I am your child still. No matter how old I get, I will always need you to watch over me. For you, God, are my permanent security blanket, my safe harbor from the storm. You are my rock, my home.

God sends an abundant amount of strength
and grace to all those who suffer.

October 5

> *[Jesus said,] "I am the good shepherd. I know my own and my own know me, just as the Father knows me and I know the Father. And I lay down my life for the sheep."*
> —John 10:14–15

I know that when I wander away from you, dear God, you always come and get me. Like a loving shepherd watching over his flock, you gently nudge me back in the right direction to keep me from harm. Sometimes I admit I refuse to listen to those nudgings, and I get into some kind of trouble because of it. But then, dear God, you always turn my attention back to you and the loving guidance you offer me. Thank you for being my shepherd, my guardian, and my heavenly Father. Amen.

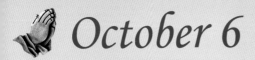# October 6

For surely I know the plans I have for you, says the Lord,
plans for your welfare and not for harm,
to give you a future with hope.
—Jeremiah 29:11

O Lord, what a comfort to know that on days when I'm frustrated and struggling to make decisions about the best use of my time, you already have a plan! Go over my "to do" list, and mark out those things I don't really need to do because they aren't a part of your plan for me. Then add anything important I may have overlooked. Teach me to trust in you, Lord, and to leave my future in your capable hands whether it is for the rest of my day or my eternal existence. Mine is a future filled with hope, and for that I am grateful beyond words.

A hopeful heart inquires, "God, what are you going to do next?"

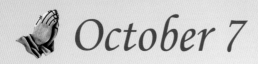

October 7

May the God of peace himself sanctify you entirely; and may your spirit and soul and body be kept sound.

—1 Thessalonians 5:23

*L*ord, help me quiet the noise of life long enough to find in that sacred silence a peace that knows no end. With all the clutter of daily life, I need all the solitude I can get to renew and refresh my spirit after a long, busy day. Your peace is the center that I can return to time and again—a place I can rest awhile and let the concerns and worries melt away. Guide me to this place of peace within me now. Amen.

The Lord hath spoken peace to my soul.

—C. E. Leslie

 # October 8

*I will seek the lost, and I will bring back the strayed, and
I will bind up the injured, and I will strengthen the weak.*

—Ezekiel 34:16

God, please forgive those in the world who do not
know what they do. Their hearts have grown cold as
stone, and they have no love for themselves or for
others. I pray for them—these people who do harm to
others—that they may somehow find hope and see the
light again and that even as they sin and sin again, that
they will repent. No human is a waste of life, and I ask
that their hearts be melted by the light of your love
and compassion and that your mercy and your forgiveness set them free.

*God's loving and forgiving spirit is
available to all his children.*

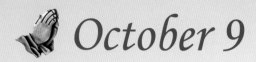# October 9

For God so loved the world that he gave his only Son,
so that everyone who believes in him may not
perish but may have eternal life.

—John 3:16

There is nothing like the feeling of being loved, Lord, and I long to find someone to love me completely for who I am. I have a heart filled with so much love to give to others, so please send me a heart that is half full, and I will give of my own to fill it. I want to be of service, and I want to give back some of the amazing grace and love you have given me. Help me find those who would most benefit from my generosity and love, and please guide me to them. Thank you, Lord.

Great thoughts come from the heart.
—Marquis de Vauvenargues

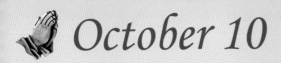

October 10

I can do all things through him who strengthens me.
—Philippians 4:13

*G*od, you are like water when I am parched with a thirst nothing else can fill. I drink of your love, and I am reborn with life force. I'm able to see everything in a different light and to make better choices when issues arise. And we both know they always do. Life is not supposed to always be easy, but with your guidance, I know that when hard times come, I can find the energy and wisdom I need to get that extra burst of hope and faith. With you, God, nothing is impossible and all things are achievable.

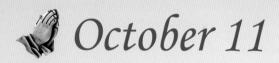

October 11

Cast all your anxiety on him, because he cares for you.

—1 Peter 5:7

O God, your love alone can fill the darkest places within my soul. Please hear my prayer, and please fill me with the light of your ever-present love. I feel utterly alone and lost, and only your grace can take away the sadness and replace it with an expectant hope and a newfound faith in your radiant goodness. The love of my family and friends helps me, but only your love, God, makes me feel whole and complete and at total peace. Please hear my prayer!

God's help is nearer than the door.

—Proverb

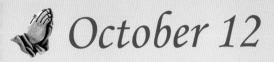# October 12

Honor your father and your mother.
—Exodus 20:12

*H*eavenly Father, today I ask you to bestow your special blessing on the elderly, especially those who are in assisted-living facilities or nursing homes. You know how hard it has been for them to give up the active lives they loved. You know the grief over losses and the fears that constantly fill their minds. And you know well the health problems with which so many of them are afflicted. Today, Lord, please bless them with a memory that brings a smile, a new sense of purpose, or an unexpected visit from a loved one. Send caretakers with the time to linger with them to see how they are truly feeling. And bless them with a deep peace that comes from knowing that they are right where they belong—in your loving hands.

The presence of the Lord is a place of help and blessing.

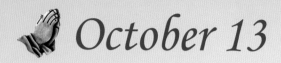 # *October 13*

Gray hair is a crown of glory; it is gained in a righteous life.
—Proverbs 16:31

*L*ord, would you think it insincere if I said thanks for
the wrinkles and gray hair? What if I said thanks for
the extra padding around my hips or for the creaking
in my knees when I climb the stairs? You see, I've come
to understand that growing older is not a right, it's a
privilege that not everyone is granted. And should you
give me the opportunity to grow gracefully into a
contented senior, with an abundance of grandchildren
and great-grandchildren, I will be blessed beyond
belief! And so I choose to replace my grumbling about
aging with gratitude for the gift. Thank you, Lord.

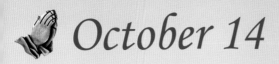 # October 14

All of you must clothe yourselves with humility in your dealings with one another.

—1 Peter 5:5

*L*ord, let me be a mentor to someone in need today. I've had my share of trials and tribulations; let me use them to help. You truly can take the ashes of our mistakes and turn them into beauty. You can work all things together for good. The worst thing that ever happened to me can become the bridge between my heart and someone else's. Thank you, Lord. In your great compassion you don't let my pain or my mistakes go to waste.

Seize opportunities to display kindness and compassion.

October 15

Keep straight the path of your feet, all your ways will be sure.

—Proverbs 4:26

O God, I cried, no dark disguise

can e'er hereafter hide from me

thy radiant identity!

Thou canst not move across the grass

But quick my eyes will see Thee pass,

Nor speak, however silently,

But my hushed voice will answer Thee.

I know the path that tells Thy way

Through the cool eve of every day;

God, I can push the grass apart

And lay my finger on Thy heart!

—Edna St. Vincent Millay

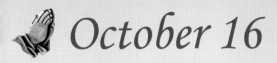# *October 16*

Jesus said [to his disciples], "Remember, I am with you always, to the end of the age."
—Matthew 28:20

*D*ear Lord, when I need you, I call your name and you are with me. You will never leave my side. You know my every desire and want before I know them myself. My faith in you is steadfast. As long as I continue to trust in you, my future is secure and no bad thing can overcome me. I ask that you watch over me as you have always done, all the days of my life.

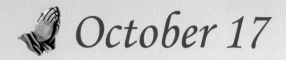 *October 17*

*I give you a new commandment, that you love one another.
Just as I have loved you, you also should love one another.*
—John 13:34

*H*eavenly Father, thank you for the grace I have received at the hands of others. I have not earned their trust or forgiveness, yet they have been given to me. Such acts of love can only be at your bidding and through your Word. Thank you for letting me long for nothing. Let me learn to love others the same way you love me, thinking only of them and not myself.

*There is only one happiness in life,
to love and be loved.*
—George Sand

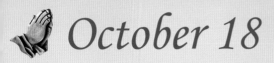

October 18

Hallelujah! For the Lord our God the Almighty reigns.
Let us rejoice and exult and give him the glory.
—Revelation 19:6–7

*T*oday, Lord, I want to be guided by a grateful heart. As I understand it, such a heart doesn't search for what's missing but delights in what's present. A grateful heart expects the best from others and gives its best in return. A grateful heart forgets what might have been and enjoys every moment of each new day as it comes. A grateful heart is a prayer of its own—one that fills the heavens with praise! Please, Lord, give me a grateful heart.

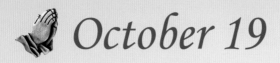 # October 19

Light is sweet, and it is pleasant for the eyes to see the sun.

—Ecclesiastes 11:7

Lord Jesus, I want to walk in your footsteps, being a beacon of love—a light, and hope for this broken world. I long to fulfill your plan for me and walk the path you have set out for me. Let me share the secret of my inner peace with all who see me by acting as you would act and loving as you would love, each and every day of my life. Amen.

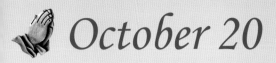

October 20

God is able to provide you with every blessing in abundance,
so that by always having enough of everything, you
may share abundantly in every good work.
—2 Corinthians 9:8

Lord, today I ask you to bless and

comfort all who daily see pain

and desperation as part of their

jobs. Bless the police officers, Lord,

and comfort them with the knowledge

that what they do truly matters. Bless

the doctors and nurses working with the seriously ill,

and comfort them with your insight. Bless and comfort

the caretakers toiling through the night, Lord, and

send your strength to restore them. All these people

are serving you as they serve others. Please give them

your special blessing. Amen.

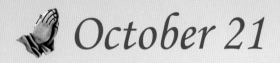 # October 21

Love is patient; love is kind . . . It does not insist
on its own way; it is not irritable or resentful.
—1 Corinthians 13:4–5

*L*ord, what an amazing thing it is that pure love keeps no record of wrongs and is not resentful! Can you teach us to love like that, Lord? Instead, we often go over and over all the grievances we have toward our spouses, children, or friends we love. Is it really possible to tear up those records and look at the people we love the way you look at us—as though we'd never sinned? I believe it is, Lord, but only by your power. Give us the strength to forget the wrongs, let go of the resentments, and embrace the love.

We should always be willing to pardon others
as many times as we pardon ourselves.

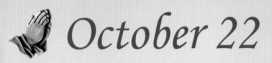 *October 22*

*Finally, all of you, have unity of spirit, sympathy, love for one
another, a tender heart, and a humble mind. Do not repay
evil for evil or abuse for abuse; but, on the contrary, repay
with a blessing. It is for this that you were called—
that you might inherit a blessing.*
—1 Peter 3:8–9

*A*lmighty God, why is it painfully difficult to forgive
the people who are closest to me? I feel that they
should love me enough to never hurt me, yet they do
so many times. Since I don't want to be bitter and
resentful, help me find the courage to forgive their
pettiness and see beyond the smallness of their behav-
ior. I know, God, that I'm not always perfect either, and
I pray they may also forgive me for hurting them, too.
We always seem to hurt the ones we love, but teach me,
God, how to forgive and be forgiven. Amen.

October 23

*If anyone is in Christ, there is a new creation: everything old
has passed away; see, everything has become new!*
—2 Corinthians 5:17

Give me a heart like yours, Lord. A heart that can show compassion and love to someone who needs it—especially when that person is incapable of showing compassion and love to me in return. This isn't something that comes naturally, Lord. We live in a society that is always asking, "What's in it for me?" Soften my heart, Lord, so that the question I always ask first is not "what's in it for me," but "what's in it for you?" Amen.

You can't give too much to a friend in need.

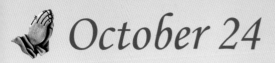

October 24

Now the word of the Lord came to me saying, "Before I formed you in the womb I knew you, and before you were born I consecrated you; I appointed you a prophet to the nations."
—Jeremiah 1:4–5

*L*ord, you knew me in my mother's womb. You set my path before me, and you watch me every moment from sunup to sundown. I need not fear any trial that I may encounter in this world because you have already written all the days of my life. All I need to do is place my trust in you and walk obediently in faith. As long as I have you to guide me, I will prevail because your holy mercy has already saved and delivered me.

No matter the worries I have, you, O God, are there ahead of me.

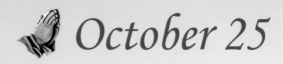

October 25

When we cry, "Abba! Father!" it is that very Spirit bearing witness with our spirit that we are children of God.

—Romans 8:15–16

*H*eavenly Father, when I was baptized, I immediately became your child, dedicated to your purpose. But you remind me again and again that we all must continue to renew ourselves and grow in relationship to you. Each day, then, be with me as I struggle to become more and more Christlike, letting go of past habits and becoming a living testament to you and your transformative powers. Amen.

Only in God do we find the blessing of renewal.

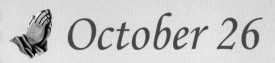

October 26

I will not leave you orphaned; I am coming to you. In a little
while the world will no longer see me, but you will see
me; because I live, you also will live.
—John 14:18–19

I don't need anything, dear Lord, but your love. For
your love is the greatest of blessings, and from it flows
all other wonderful things. The love that knows no
limitations is all I desire, for peace, prosperity, and joy
are found in that love. Your love, Lord, is a cup of the
sweetest wine, which quenches my thirst. Your love,
Lord, is manna from heaven, which fills and satisfies
my hunger. I am loved and blessed, and that is all I
need, dear Lord.

Love is the best of all reasons for living.

October 27

There is no Holy God like the Lord, no one besides you;
there is no Rock like our God.

—1 Samuel 2:2

*H*eavenly Father, I put my faith in you, for you are my rock and my foundation. I know that upon you I can always stand firm, even as the ground surrounding me shakes and trembles. I will not fall, for your arms embrace me faithfully, and I will not have to deal with my challenges alone. It is good to know I am always cared for and that even when things look as though they are falling apart, with my faith in you, I will soon see that my life is really coming together. My faith in you makes me strong, God. Thank you.

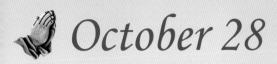# October 28

To set the mind on the flesh is death, but to set the mind on the Spirit is life and peace.

—Romans 8:6

O Lord, you are so good to me. What a gift it is that when I first bow my head to ask you to quiet my spirit and give me peace, you are already at work doing just that! Somehow, knowing I am in your presence, the issues and situations that seemed particularly difficult just a short time ago lose importance—especially when seen in the light of the peace you always have to offer. Thank you, Lord, that I can come to you in such a frazzled state and lift my head after praying, restored by your peace. You are so good.

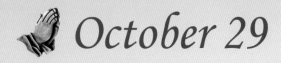

October 29

Humble yourselves before the Lord, and he will exalt you.

—James 4:10

*G*od in heaven, you are my hope from above, and you
alone can lift my spirits and make me see that behind
the clouds there is still a sun shining strong and bright.
I am having a tough time believing in myself right now,
and I ask that you bear me up on wings of eagles and
carry me away from the heaviness of my burdens for
just a little while. In prayer, I feel the promise of your
peace, and I know that hope is still there waiting to
break through the clouds and shine into my life again.

*God and God alone gives us hope when there
seems no end to our suffering.*

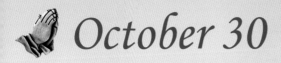

October 30

Come to me, all you that are weary and are carrying heavy burdens, and I will give you rest. Take my yoke upon you, and learn from me; for I am gentle and humble in heart, and you will find rest for your souls.
—Matthew 11:28–29

Dear God, I pray today that you will always be by my side like a best friend or constant companion, walking with me throughout my life. I pray that I can always turn to you with my troubles and talk to you about my concerns, for I know that you will never turn away from me. I pray that I can always count on your love to lift me up when the weight of the world drags me down. I pray with a humble heart and in the name of Jesus. Amen.

Life becomes much easier when we know we are never alone.

October 31

*You shall love the Lord your God with all your heart, and
with all your soul, and with all your might.*

—Deuteronomy 6:5

*L*ord, I truly want to love you with all my heart, soul,
mind, and strength—so why do I have such a hard
time doing it? At times my heart is fully engaged in
loving you, but my mind is struggling with unanswered
questions. Some days my soul seems too weary to love,
Lord. And my strength? Well, it's just not
there. Forgive me, Lord. It is my
deepest desire to love you as
totally as you deserve to be loved.
Help me even in this, Lord.

We were made to love and to be loved.

My Prayer Life

_____

_____

_____

_____

_____

_____

_____

_____

_____

_____

_____

_____

_____

_____

_____

_____

_____

_____

_____

_____

_____

# November 1

*[Jesus] said, "Blessed rather are those who hear
the word of God and obey it!"*
—Luke 11:28

*L*ord God, I am truly blessed to know you. To be able
to read your Word and talk with you and hear your
voice is nothing short of a miracle. I thank you for
choosing me to be your child. My relationship with
you and your Son, Jesus Christ, is what makes my life
wonderful and worthwhile. I hope for
nothing more than to continue
to grow closer to you, day by day.
Thank you for loving me.

*Reasons to rejoice and give
thanks are endless.*

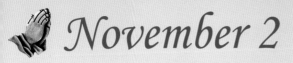

November 2

This is the day that the Lord has made;
let us rejoice and be glad in it.
—Psalm 118:24

*L*ord, I want to go through my day
energized by thankfulness. Help me be
generous and not selfish with unpleasant
people. Remind me that shortfalls can be
windfalls when I learn to appreciate what I have
and not focus on what I don't have. Seal this attitude
of gratitude in my heart, dear Lord, that I may draw
others closer to you. Make me a reflection of your
glory and a person with a grateful heart.

Gratitude is an attitude of loving what you
have, and this undoubtedly leads
to contentment.

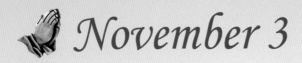 # November 3

> *We bring you good news, that you should turn . . . to the living*
> *God, who made the heavens and the earth and*
> *the sea and all that is in them.*
> —Acts 14:15

God, today I pray not for myself but for all the living things you have made on this great green earth. My hope is that we will show compassion to the creatures of the sky, the sea, and the land for all that they provide for us. May we respect and admire their unique beauty and purpose. May we learn to treat them with respect and dignity. And may we learn to take better care of the planet we call home, having compassion for life in all its wondrous and miraculous forms.

Be thankful for all of creation.

November 4

The only thing that counts is faith working through love.
—Galatians 5:6

*D*ear God, sometimes I wonder if you just shake your head when you see our meager attempts to help others. So often we are giving them just what they need to survive the day, but holding back in terms of offering them the abundance that can be theirs through faith in you. When we reach out to others in love, God, let us also reach out with faith and be willing to share the faith that sustains us. Then and only then will all their needs be met. In your Son's most precious name, I pray. Amen.

 *November 5*

Do not remember the former things, or consider the things of old. I am about to do a new thing; . . . I will make a way in the wilderness and rivers in the desert.

—Isaiah 43:18–19

*A*lmighty God, I seem to have lost my sense of direction lately. I keep repeating the same mistakes, and I always seem to be banging up against the same obstacles over and over again. I could use some direction—that is, some insight to help me learn what I'm supposed to learn from my troubles—so I don't make the same mistakes. I pray that you will show me the steps along the way and that you will constantly adjust my path with your wisdom and loving kindness. Thank you, God.

God provides signposts to help us find our way along this ever-changing journey.

November 6

O my God, . . . We do not present our supplication
before you on the ground of our righteousness,
but on the ground of your great mercies.
—Daniel 9:18

$\mathcal{D}$ear Lord, I humbly admit that I've been withholding certain parts of my life, thinking I could maintain my earthly ways and still be dedicated to you. But I'm finding again and again that your grace cannot truly change me until I sacrifice every bit of myself up to you. I want to become new in Christ, and so I come to you today to offer all of my life to you, as a living sacrifice to your kingdom. Take me and mold me into what you desire, Lord, making me forever transformed by your love. Amen.

When we fill our days with the noisy blur of
constant activity, we miss the gifts and
blessings of silence and stillness.

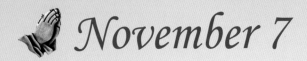

November 7

Restore to me the joy of your salvation,
and sustain in me a willing spirit.
—Psalm 51:12

*S*ometimes, God, I feel like a withered-up plant in desperate need of sunshine and water, but there seems to be neither in sight. Then I remember my source, and I turn to the warmth of your love to be replenished and renewed and to open my heart to the sun again. Like rain, you quench my thirst and wash away my fears. Your loving light scatters the darkness I stumble about in. I feel that I can hold my head up high again, in the renewing grace of your presence in my life.

November 8

One who is slow to anger is better than the mighty, and one whose temper is controlled than one who captures a city.
—Proverbs 16:32

*H*eavenly Father, I want to forgive. My mind tells my heart to let go of the past, but I just can't. My human weakness makes me remember every slight and misdeed done to me. Lord, help me release the hurt and anger and move to the place of acceptance. I want to soften my hardened heart and create a new relationship, one that is built on love and trust and one that is consecrated to you. Amen.

Let your anger set with the sun and not rise again with it.
—Irish Proverb

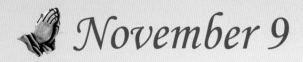

November 9

*Surely God is my salvation; I will trust, and will not be
afraid, for the Lord God is my strength and my
might; he has become my salvation.*

—Isaiah 12:2

*H*oly God, even in times of fear and uncertainty,
please remind me that you always surround me. With
every breath I take, let me breathe in your merciful
love. With every blink of my eyes, let me see your
comforting presence. With every beat of
my heart, let me feel your Spirit
envelop me. I ask that you make
me yours, totally and completely, Lord, and let me rest
in the loving refuge of your
arms. Amen.

# November 10

[Jesus] rebuked the wind, and said to the sea, "Peace! Be still!" Then the wind ceased, and there was a dead calm.
—Mark 4:39

You calmed the stormy waters, Lord, and quieted the thunderous skies. I ask you to calm the stormy waters for me as I struggle with the challenges I face. I know that with the peace you provide, I can face any obstacle and get through any trial or tribulation before me. In the stillness within, you wait for me, always present, always ready to bring me safely back home as a lighthouse guides a ship through the cold, dark fog to the comfort of the shore. Thank you for calming my storms, God.

In all human sorrows nothing gives comfort but love and faith.
—Leo Tolstoy

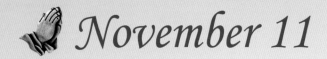 *November 11*

[Jesus] is the mediator of a new covenant, so that those who are called may receive the promised eternal inheritance, because a death has occurred that redeems them from the transgressions under the first covenant.

—Hebrews 9:15

Lord Jesus, through your grace, you have removed my transgressions as far from me as the farthest star. Still, I feel the scars and hurts of my past. I have hurt others, I have hurt you, and I have hurt myself. You forgive me in your boundless mercy, and I pray that you will help me forgive myself. I want to move forward freely, healed and whole, reborn in your love.

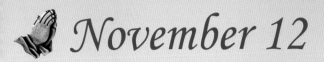

November 12

Like a horse in the desert, they did not stumble. Like cattle
that go down into the valley, the spirit of the Lord
gave them rest. Thus you led your people,
to make for yourself a glorious name.
—Isaiah 63:13–14

𝒟ear Lord, please show me how I can get on the right path, for I have lost my way. I can't seem to do anything right lately, and it feels as though I'm going against the wind and being pushed back two steps for every one step forward I take. I need your guidance to point me in the right direction so that I can get back on track again. I trust you alone to lead me where I need to be right now in my life, and so I surrender my will to yours. Please guide me, and I will follow wherever you lead me. Thank you, Lord.

Nothing about God's children is too trivial
or ordinary, too overwhelming or
dreadful for God to care about.

 *November 13*

*Thus he has given us, through these things,
his precious and very great promises.*

—2 Peter 1:4

*W*hat wonderful, bountiful blessings
you have given to me, my God!
Indeed, you have filled my life with
what is truly amazing, truly awesome,
and truly inspiring. Oh, I know there
have been challenges, and I'm sure there will
be more. And yet, when I look at all the positive things
in life, I believe in my heart that I can conquer the
darkness along my path and find even newer blessings
around the bend. Thank you, God, for showing me
that your promises are steadfast and true, and your
blessings are never-ending. Amen.

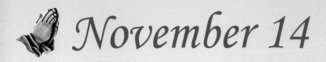

November 14

When he saw the crowds, he had compassion for them.
—Matthew 9:36

I want my heart to be more like yours, Lord. I want a heart that sees the need before it's expressed, the hurt before the tears flow, and the pain even before the wound is inflicted. How many times a day do I walk by someone who could use a hand, a word, even a smile and totally miss the opportunity to be your representative on earth? Open the eyes of my heart, Lord. Let your compassion go with me wherever I go.

God sometimes uses our hands
to comfort those in need.

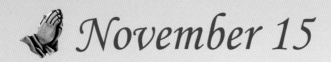

November 15

[Jesus said,] "Let the little children come to me;"...And he
took them up in his arms, laid his hands
on them, and blessed them.

—Mark 10:14, 16

*L*ord, today I ask you to be with all
the parents-to-be who secretly
worry, "What if I don't love this
baby when it's born?" What a
surprise they have in store, Lord!
For from your overflowing bounty
of love you always deliver a generous
portion to each one. And when the second
baby comes? You simply double the capacity
for love. Thank you, Lord, for a parent's love.
Something that pure and precious could only come
from you.

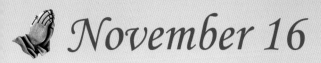

November 16

It is good to give thanks to the Lord.

—Psalm 92:1

*L*ord, I need to confess something today. In spite of all the riches you've given me, I sometimes find myself wanting something someone else has—that perfect job, a larger house, or even those great-looking shoes. Forgive me for being ungrateful, Lord. You have blessed me in so many ways. You have given me riches beyond compare through your Son, Jesus Christ. Please decrease my envy, Lord, and increase my gratitude. Amen.

# November 17

Jesus said to them, "I am the bread of life. Whoever comes to me will never be hungry, and whoever believes in me will never be thirsty."
—John 6:35

God, sometimes I feel like a stale loaf of bread, as if I am living the same day over and over. I feel tired and resigned to living half a life, just getting by. I pray you will light a fire within me and reignite in me the interests and passions I once had that made my life so unique and filled with delight. Rekindle my desire to be better each day, to not settle for less, and to lift my eyes upward to what is possible, not downward to what is impossible. Fill me with a newfound purpose, that I may become as new as freshly baked bread.

It's never too late to be a joyful explorer.

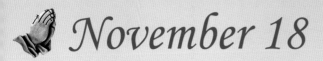

November 18

Let us hold fast to the confession of our hope without
wavering, for he who has promised is faithful.
—Hebrews 10:23

$\mathcal{D}$ear God, there isn't much in this world of which
we can be absolutely sure. We're one meeting with
the boss away from losing our job in a layoff and one
phone call from the doctor away from finding out our
health is seriously compromised. Our children can
disappoint us, and even marriages can become shaky.
We have no guarantees about our finances, and even
the most expensive automobile is likely to break down
sometime. So where is our security? Where should we
place our trust? O, Lord, we praise you because we
know it is in you. You and you alone will never change,
and you will never disappoint us. You are always faithful, Lord, and so we place all our hope in you and
your promises.

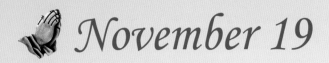

November 19

Then the angel showed me the river of the water of life, bright as crystal, flowing from the throne of God and of the Lamb.

—Revelation 22:1

Lord Jesus, it is too easy to seek comfort from material things—from a new car or sofa, from a trip to the mall or to the movies. But you are not found in worldly things. The only true source of everlasting comfort is your love—the living water you offer us from your very lips. Let me remember to seek first your will, perfect and divine. It is only then that my weary heart will rest and find sanctuary. Amen.

November 20

O give thanks to the Lord, for he is good;
for his steadfast love endures forever.

—1 Chronicles 16:34

*N*ow thank we all our God

with hearts and hands and voices,

who wondrous things hath done,

in whom his world rejoices;

who, from our mothers' arms,

hath blessed us on our way

with countless gifts of love,

and still is ours today.

—Martin Rinkart,
translated by Catherine Winkworth,
"Now Thank We All Our God"

November 21

O Lord, hear; O Lord, forgive; O Lord,
listen and act and do not delay!
—Daniel 9:19

*H*eavenly Father, I made a mess of this relationship, and I ask to be forgiven. I did my best, but it wasn't enough to overcome the challenges we faced, and I know that I have done my share of hurting just as I have been hurt. Please find it in your heart to forgive me, and help me be forgiven by those I have harmed. And please, God, help me forgive myself. I learned a valuable lesson in this situation, and now it is time to let go of the pain and heal.

They who forgive most shall be most forgiven.
— William Blake

November 22

Jesus Christ is the same yesterday and today and forever.
—Hebrews 13:8

My heavenly Father, there are few aspects of our lives that are constant. The political scene shifts with each election. Careers seem to be heading in a positive direction and then abruptly end. Fortunes rise and fall. Even relationships sometimes reach their peaks and then fade away. But you, O Lord, never change! Your power and your majesty always were and always will be. Thank you, Lord, that when we put our faith in you, we are never disappointed.

Faith does not fear change, but knows that all change is simply the Spirit's way of moving our life in the direction of our destiny.

# November 23

For it is better to suffer for doing good, if suffering should be God's will, than to suffer for doing evil.

—1 Peter 3:17

*E*ven the suffering in my life has been a blessing in disguise, dear Lord, and the lessons I have learned have given me the wisdom and understanding to live better and be a better person. I am a stronger, more resilient person because of the obstacles you have placed before me, all of which have brought me countless blessings once I made it to the other side. Though I prefer not to suffer, I know it is a part of life and one that can often lead to the sweetest of blessings.

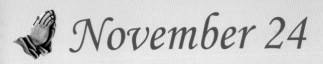

November 24

Clothe yourselves with compassion, kindness,
humility, meekness, and patience.

—Colossians 3:12

You did it, Lord! I asked you to be with me at lunch today and you were— helping me to compassionately listen to a person I've often found difficult to be around. She must have noticed, Lord. Because you filled my heart with compassion for her, I was able to focus intently on what she was saying and simply give her the gift of listening. Thanks for going to lunch with me, Lord. When you're along, it makes all the difference.

With God's guidance, I can help others
and give more.

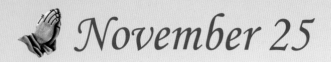
November 25

God opposes the proud, but gives grace to the humble.
—James 4:6

*L*ord, let us never miss the glimpses of grace you put in the simplest of places and deeds. A visit with an old friend in a nursing home can be bathed in your grace. A brief exchange with someone in line can deliver a blessed amount of your grace into their day. Open our eyes to all the creative ways you are sending your grace into our world, Lord. And don't let us miss the glimpses ourselves.

Faith is a living, daring confidence in God's grace.
—Martin Luther

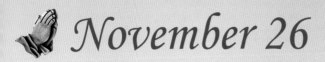

November 26

Be strong and courageous; do not be frightened or dismayed,
for the Lord your God is with you wherever you go.

—Joshua 1:9

*L*ord, you are the only one we need. Like a little child who wakes up crying in the middle of the night, cold and scared, we long to be comforted. But you wrap your arms around us and keep us safe in the shelter of your love. And so we come to you as desperate children again and again, wanting nothing more than to gaze into your face and receive your comfort. Thank you for the promise that we are your children forever and that when we come to you for comfort, you will never turn us away.

When the quiet after the storm finally comes
to our hearts, we look up to find that
God is surely with us.

# November 27

I will both lie down and sleep in peace; for you alone,
O Lord, make me lie down in safety.
—Psalm 4:8

*H*eavenly Father, please bring peace to the relationships in my life. Some of the toughest challenges I have
as a Christian involve my relationships with others.
Even though we are brothers and sisters in Christ, we
struggle to love each other and to treat each other with
patience and loving kindness. Today, please bless me
with an extra dose of inner calm, that I might retain
my composure and remember your laws as I am dealing with others. I long to do what is right, and I know
that with your help, I can keep your commandment
to love others. I ask in Jesus' name. Amen.

November 28

Then I heard the voice of the Lord saying,
"Whom shall I send, and who will go for us?"
And I said, "Here am I; send me!"

—Isaiah 6:8

*H*oly God, you are truly merciful and caring! You have filled me entirely with your love that I cannot help but share it with others. I go through my days, amazed that you have chosen me to help spread your Word. I delight in helping others learn of your power and truth. I am truly blessed by your existence, and I long to praise your name, letting others see the glory of the miracles you have worked in me.

Our Christian fervor can be measured by
our desire to grow in love.

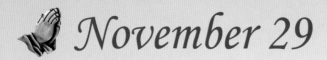

November 29

Indeed, you are my lamp, O Lord,
the Lord lightens my darkness.
—2 Samuel 22:29

*H*eavenly Father, I come to you to beg for guidance. I'm at the end of my human understanding, and I don't know which way to turn, other than to turn to you. Please place your hand on me and give me the wisdom to make the right choices. I am lost and scared, and I need you to help me find my way again. Shine on my path so that I can see the pitfalls ahead, and light my way so that I can walk safely.

November 30

As his anointing teaches you about all things, and is true
and is not a lie, and just as it has taught you, abide in him.

—1 John 2:27

Dear God, why are we so anxious
to take things into our own hands
while waiting on you and hoping that
you will take care of our problems?
Teach us to wait actively, Lord, by abiding in
you until we know which way you want us to go.
Then let us tirelessly take off in that direction,
confident that you are the wind beneath our wings.
Keep us from leaving without you, Lord. We want to
journey through this life energetically and purpose-
fully, and that sometimes means waiting for you. Amen.

God knows what is best and has
my highest good in mind.

My Prayer Life

_____
_____
_____
_____
_____
_____
_____
_____
_____
_____
_____
_____
_____
_____
_____
_____
_____
_____
_____
_____
_____
_____
_____

 *December 1*

Do not be conformed to this world, but be transformed by the renewing of your minds, so that you may discern what is the will of God—what is good and acceptable and perfect.

—Romans 12:2

*A*fter another night of mindless television, Lord, I lie in bed and try to erase the images and thoughts swirling through my head. Why do we fall into the trap of wasting time this way? When I think of all the wonderful books I haven't read or the time I could have invested in people and in my family instead of actors in sitcoms, I feel ashamed. Renew my mind, Lord. Fill it with thoughts of you, with images of eternal glory, and with your restoring words of Scripture. Watch over me as I sleep, Lord, and let me wake refreshed—with the knowledge that you can and will direct my mind in the ways you would have it go.

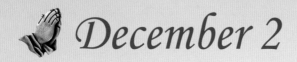

December 2

Now to him who is able to keep you from falling, and to make you stand without blemish in the presence of his glory with rejoicing, to the only God our Savior, through Jesus Christ our Lord, be glory, majesty, power, and authority, before all time and now and forever. Amen.

—Jude 24–25

*T*oday, I sing out in praise for the Lord has made me whole. My life is filled with peace and balance, and harmony is the order of my day. My life was not always like this. I once took on way more than I should have, and it wore me down. But in God's love I now stand restored and at peace with whatever each new day brings. I know in my heart that I can handle anything as long as I am connected to the source that is my God. It is a source from which I can find all the highest and best blessings life has to offer. It is a source of pure and eternal peace.

To have true inner peace, we must release everything to God.

December 3

*Pay attention to what you hear; the measure you give will be
the measure you get, and still more will be given you.*
—Mark 4:24

*H*oly God, when I am depressed and down, it is hard
to see the good in my life. I am so focused on the bad
that I can't see beyond my troubles. Instead, help me
shift my eyes to focus on the good things and to see
the world as a glass half full rather than half empty. Lift
my heart from the pit of gloom and
show me the light again that I may
recognize just how much you
have blessed me and continue
to bless me each day. Amen.

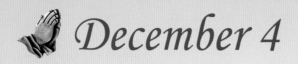# December 4

*Truly I tell you, just as you did it to one of the least of these
who are members of my family, you did it to me.*
—Matthew 25:40

God, thank you for the ability to serve others and fulfill their needs. Whether I'm lending a hand, sharing a kind word, or providing a meal, when I help another person and see gratitude in their eyes, I know I am doing your work here on earth. Please help me recognize all the opportunities I have to serve so that I can give back a small fraction of the many blessings you have given me.

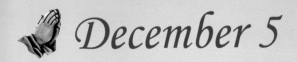

December 5

At that time I will bring you home, at the time when I gather
you; for I will make you renowned and praised among
all the peoples of the earth, when I restore your
fortunes before your eyes, says the Lord.
—Zephaniah 3:20

When all hope is lost, or so it seems in my heart, you, dear Lord, remind me to never give up and never give in. Like a candle that burns eternally, you relight the flame of hope within, and I feel a new sense of power and certainty that all things can be overcome. To know that I always have hope is to know that life can always get better, sometimes even in the blink of an eye, if I just surrender to your will and hold on tight. Thank you, Lord, for the everlasting hope that fills my heart.

People of hope ascend hills and mountains
others have declared impossible.

December 6

Blessed are the peacemakers, for they will be
called children of God.
—Matthew 5:9

*A*lmighty God, how awesome you are to conceive
of forgiveness in a world so fraught with sin and evil.
Today I ask you to be with all those who are struggling
to forgive someone for an unspeakable grievance. Even
when they know that it is only when they forgive that
they will be free of the pain, some acts are really hard
to forgive. I think of the parents whose children have
been kidnapped or murdered, the wife who has been
abused, and the innocent victims of a drunk driver.
Lord, give all these people your power to forgive so
that their pain and anger won't become a sickness in
their souls, for they won't be able to do it without you.

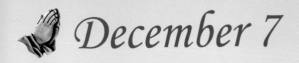

December 7

*I pray that you may have the power to comprehend, with all
the saints, what is the breadth and length and height
and depth, and to know the love of Christ that
surpasses knowledge, so that you may be
filled with all the fullness of God.*
—Ephesians 3:18–19

I know you love me, Lord! I feel your presence today
as I work. I see your answer to last week's prayer right
before my eyes. I feel my spirit lifted when I sing
praises to you as I drive in the car. You are behind me,
before me, and in me. Wherever I go, I am surrounded
by your love—love that knows
no bounds and has no end.
Thank you, Lord. All I can
say is, "I love you, too!"

*Celebrate love, for it is
the breath of your existence.*

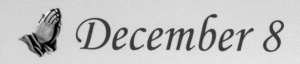 *December 8*

Let justice roll down like waters, and righteousness like an ever-flowing stream.
—Amos 5:24

*A*lmighty God, overseer of all that exists, do you see the needs of the poor and displaced children of the world? I know you do, Lord, but I sometimes wonder how you can allow them to live without safe water to drink or shelter from the raging storms and blazing heat. Comfort them, Lord, and if my discomfort when I think of them is a sign that there is something I can do to help, I am willing. Please show me the way.

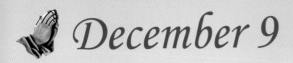

December 9

He heals the brokenhearted, and binds up their wounds.

—Psalm 147:3

*O*God, my spirit is shattered! I cannot even begin to put the millions of pieces back together. I am scared that everything I hold dear will be taken from me, and I will be left loveless and broken. I turn to your Word for solace, and you tell me to keep steady in my faith. If I remain true to you, recovery will come, day by day, with your help. Please be with me in this dark period, giving me comfort and reassuring me of your presence. I ask in Jesus' precious name. Amen.

The principal part of faith is patience.
—George MacDonald

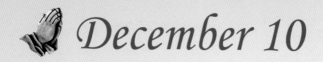

December 10

Sin will have no dominion over you, since you are
not under law but under grace.

—Romans 6:14

I know it's true, Lord. Because of your presence in my life, the sins that had so much control over me in the past aren't the least bit enticing anymore. You orchestrated that change in me by your grace, and I thank you. I thank you, too, that you didn't create a long list of laws for me to follow, knowing full well I couldn't keep them all perfectly. Instead, you simply asked me to believe in you and receive the abundant provision of your grace. What a wonderful, awesome way to save me, Lord! I thank you with my whole heart—and with my life. Amen.

When it seems as though God is treating you
like a favorite child, that's grace.

December 11

Be patient, therefore, beloved, until the coming of the Lord.

—James 5:7

O God, though you are silent today, I believe you will answer my prayers for guidance and help. I'm sure that you have heard my pleas, and you know what my heart desires, but more than that, you know what is best for me. I am willing to wait until I hear your voice and until your meaning is clear to me. I will have patience, for I have faith that all things happen according to your plan.

We must believe that the Lord knows what is truly best for us.

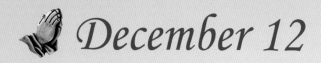

December 12

Let us love, not in word or speech, but in truth and action.

—1 John 3:18

*L*ord, only you can love unconditionally. Try as we might, we fall back into loving based on performance or loving based on being loved in return. Why do we make love a competition or an equation? Your love for us is unqualified, completely accessible, and eternal. Dwell in our hearts and minds Lord, and direct our actions toward others. Help us move ever closer to the unconditional way of loving that can change the world one heart at a time.

December 13

The Lord is my light and my salvation; . . .
The Lord is the stronghold of my life.
—Psalm 27:1

*L*ook upon us, O Lord, and let all
the darkness of our souls vanish before
the beams of thy brightness. Fill us with
holy love, and open to us the treasures of thy wisdom.
All our desire is known unto thee, therefore perfect
what thou hast begun, and what thy Spirit has awak-
ened us to ask in prayer. We seek thy face. Turn thy
face unto us and show us thy glory. Then shall our
longing be satisfied, and our peace shall be perfect.
—Saint Augustine

Nothing more is required than this:
receive your good gifts from above.

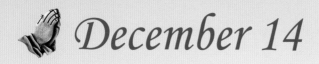

December 14

The Lord, your God, is in your midst, a warrior who gives
victory; he will rejoice over you with gladness,
he will renew you in his love.

—Zephaniah 3:17

*T*oday, heavenly Father, I pray for a little more grace in my life. I could use some help from above—some small miracles today to remind me of the good in life and that I'm loved and cared for. Please send down your special grace to me, enough for just today, for tomorrow will take care of itself. An angel or two will do, but even if you could just spare a bit of divine guidance, I would be forever grateful. I don't need much, Father. Just a little bit of grace will do. Thank you!

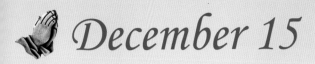

December 15

When the Advocate comes, whom I will send to you from the Father, the Spirit of truth who comes from the Father, he will testify on my behalf.

—John 15:26

O God, my heavenly Father, thank you for sending your Holy Spirit to be with us and guide our decisions. Because I can carry this constant reminder of your love within my heart, I'm never far from you. If I'm ever confused or uncertain, I just pray and then listen for that still, small voice of yours to confirm that my choice is the one you would have me make. Thank you, Lord, for not forsaking us or leaving us to our own earthly devices. Your love for us is truly great!

God directs my thoughts and guides my actions.

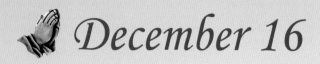

December 16

Truly I tell you, unless you change and become like children, you will never enter the kingdom of heaven. Whoever becomes humble like this child is the greatest in the kingdom of heaven.

—Matthew 18:3–4

*J*ust as children have faith in their parents to love them and watch over them, I have faith in you, heavenly Father, to always love me, too. I look up to you for wisdom and guidance, and I pray to you for patience and understanding. You always come through for me in wondrous ways, proving to me that my faith is well placed. As your beloved child, I feel nourished and protected by your love, and I will always believe in you, Lord, just as you always believe in me. Amen.

Keep the Lord close.

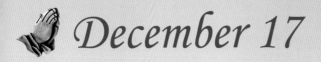

December 17

*Love ... bears all things, believes all things,
hopes all things, endures all things.*
—1 Corinthians 13:4, 7

*F*ather in heaven, thank you for creating the kind of
love that can hope all things. Without that kind of love,
a new mother of a disabled child wouldn't have the
strength to get up in the morning. Without that special
kind of love, the young spouse of a deployed soldier
wouldn't have the courage to make plans for "when he
gets home." A love that hopes is a love that knows you
are in control. It's a love that knows that when we place
our hope in you, our love can endure any and all
circumstances. We are able to hope all things because
we love you and you love us. Thank you, Father.

*Our hope is in the goodness
and justice and power of God.*

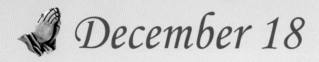

December 18

I will send down the showers in their season;
they shall be showers of blessing.

—Ezekiel 34:26

*O*Lord, how we anticipate and welcome
your life-giving rain on our parched
land! What a blessing it is when you
open your storehouses and send us
the right amount of moisture to make our crops grow
and our rivers flow! I know there are blessings in every
season, but it's harder to be grateful for the dry times.
Even then you are with us, and so we still thank you for
the blessing of water. How it refreshes us!

To embrace the gifts each day brings is to
acknowledge that the Creator never
walks away from his creation.

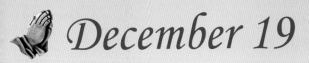# December 19

Rejoice with those who rejoice, weep with those who weep.
—Romans 12:15

O Lord, I know that true compassion is seeing into the heart of another and sharing in what they are feeling. Help me be better at doing that, Lord. Give me your insight into what's really going on in their hearts and minds. Still my mind and my agenda, and let me truly be in tune with what the people you've put in my life are feeling. And, Lord, keep me from trying to change or fix things. Help me to simply come alongside them and be happy for them or cry with them. Remind me, always, that showing true compassion is never, never about me or my feelings. You modeled compassion so well for us, Lord. May it be visible in me. Amen.

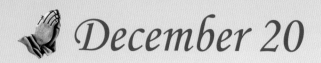

December 20

Beloved, do not imitate what is evil but imitate what is good.
—3 John 11

God, of all your precious gifts, love is the rarest and most precious of all. Too often I find myself acting in ways that are unloving and unkind. That is when I most need your love to remind me to stop and take a deep breath. Anger and hatred never solve any problems. Only love seems to make the rough spots smoother and the hard roads easier to walk upon. I ask that you continue to remind me of the power of love each day, especially when it seems so much easier to choose to be unkind.

Cooperating with God will permit us to generously pass on to others some of the many blessings from his rich storehouse.

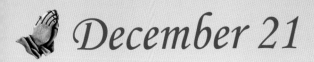# December 21

Surely goodness and mercy shall follow me all the days of my life, and I shall dwell in the house of the Lord my whole life long.

—Psalm 23:6

*H*eavenly God, I thank you that even in the depths of my deepest pain, I can still feel your presence and love. Even when all seems bleak and dark, through your holy words, I know that I am never really alone. Because of your Son, Jesus Christ, I am protected for all eternity. This assurance allows me hope, and I am so thankful that I am saved by your mercy and redeemed by your love. Amen.

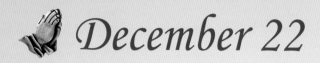

December 22

Jesus answered her, "If you knew the gift of God, and who it is that is saying to you, 'Give me a drink,' you would have asked him, and he would have given you living water."

—John 4:10

*O*Lord, how precious is the water that flows down from the mountains to restore our land after a long drought! Thank you for sending the fresh, life-giving water to nourish our lawns, our flowerbeds, and our bodies. Yet, as desirable as that water is, Lord, we know that the living water we receive from you is the most precious of all. Thank you, Lord, for sending your living water to refresh our parched souls. We stand in the rejuvenating stream of your love and grace.

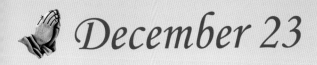

December 23

We have gifts that differ according to the grace given to us.

—Romans 12:6

*C*reator God, how wise of you to make us all intriguingly different and to send a variety of gifts into the world through us! How boring it would be if everyone in one church had the gift of preaching, but no one had the gift of hospitality! How ineffective your church would be if no one had the gifts of serving or mercy as well! But by your grace we have different gifts. We thank you for them all, God, and we ask you to forgive us when we don't use them as freely as we should.

We are all one in Jesus Christ.

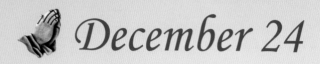

December 24

*When you turn to the right or you turn to the left, your
ears shall hear a word behind you, saying,
"This is the way; walk in it."*
—Isaiah 30:21

*D*ear Lord, so often we are on a road that's full of
potholes and unexpected hazards, and we question
why you sent us in this particular direction. But looking back, we often realize that it was that rocky road
you took us down that led us to a place we needed to
be—a place selected and ordained by you. Thank you,
Lord, for being with us on that difficult road and for
telling us which way to go to avoid total disaster. We
have learned that you truly do work all things together
for good, and so we will take the rough road that leads
us ever closer to you.

*It is exactly at the point of our deepest despair
that God is closest.*

December 25

The Lord does not see as mortals see; they look on the outward appearance, but the Lord looks on the heart.

—1 Samuel 16:7

*F*ather in heaven, if ever I feel far from you, I just need to quiet my mind and heart and wait for you to speak—particularly on this special day, during which we celebrate the earthly birth of your beloved Son! You are always with me, but sometimes your voice gets drowned out by the rush of this busy season. Your faithful presence is constant, however, and if I look deeply enough, I will find you. And when I do, you are always waiting to welcome me home. Let me return to you again and again, especially today.
I pray in the name of my savior,
Jesus Christ. Amen.

Only when we trust God, do we have peace and assurance in the shelter of his care.

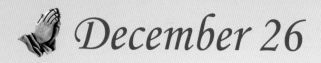

December 26

*Can any idols of the nations bring rain? Or can the heavens
give showers? Is it not you, O Lord our God? We set
our hope on you, for it is you who do all this.*

—Jeremiah 14:22

I gave up hope, dear God, and then you came to me.
I gave up faith, dear God, and you whispered in my ear
that all was not lost. I gave up love, dear God, and you
washed over me with a wave of the love that knows no
bounds. I gave up peace, dear God, and you filled me
with a peace that goes beyond understanding. Thank
you for keeping hope alive in my heart and my soul.
Dear God, with hope restored, my faith and love and
peace are sure to follow.

*Hope is the gentle urging of the soul when the
mind, heart, and body are too tired to go on.*

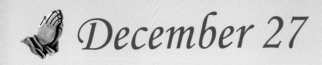# December 27

Love your enemies, do good to those who hate you, bless those
who curse you, pray for those who abuse you.
—Luke 6:27–28

My Lord, you instructed us to forgive our enemies,
but I need a little extra courage to do that today. I want
to hold on to my anger like a weapon, but in my heart
I know that I am just hurting myself by doing so. I pray
for some strength and fortitude to face my responsibilities for what happened and to accept what
others did in kind. I pray to forgive
those who have betrayed me, even
as I ask them to forgive me for my
role in this situation. Help me,
Lord, to forgive them.

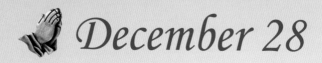

December 28

Do to others as you would have them do to you.
—Luke 6:31

*T*hose times when I most need some loving kindness, God, are when I most need to give someone else that same kindness. For there is one lesson I have learned, and that is to give is to receive. What we put forward comes back to us in the end. Today, I will set aside my problems and reach out to someone who has bigger challenges to face, knowing that even as I help that person, I am helping myself. I will spread love and openly receive love with a willing and grateful heart.

The language of an open and loving heart is often heard in the quietest, most simple of gestures.

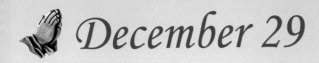

December 29

A friend loves at all times.
—Proverbs 17:17

*F*ather in heaven, how glad I am that you put so many precious friends in my life over the years. When I look back through time I can still see their faces and remember their encouragement and love, even if time and distance have separated us. Never let me take

my friends for granted, Lord.

I praise and thank you for

the ones I've known and

the ones I've yet to meet.

Friendship is one of your

greatest gifts, and I'm truly

glad you thought of it.

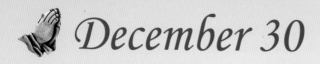

December 30

Let us therefore approach the throne of grace with boldness,
so that we may receive mercy and find grace
to help in time of need.
—Hebrews 4:16

My Lord, too often we are timid when it comes to bringing our requests before you, but we know that we have complete access to the holy of holies. So embolden us, Lord! Teach us to accept that the grace we have been given is powerful now, not just some day when we are united with you. We boldly lift up prayers to you, asking for justice, righteousness, and peace in our world, Lord. By your grace we humbly ask you to listen and to act.

December 31

We are the clay, and you are our potter;
we are all the work of your hand.
—Isaiah 64:8

O God, you created us, and you know us better than
we know ourselves. You also love us more than we love
ourselves—and more than anyone on this earth loves
us. Resting in that truth, I know that it's easier to turn
our lives over to you. When we need to be redirected,
we trust you to do the redirecting. When we're bent
out of shape, we know you will be the one to straighten
us out again. And if things ever get so bad that you
need to humble us and remold us, even then we place
ourselves in your hands. For what you create by your
hands is always more magnificent than what we can
design ourselves. Thank you, Lord. Amen.

For great is your love, reaching to the heavens.

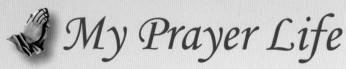

My Prayer Life

_____

_____

_____

_____

_____

_____

_____

_____

_____

_____

_____

_____

_____

_____

_____

_____

_____

_____

_____

_____

ACKNOWLEDGMENTS:

Cover Art: Shutterstock

Artville, Brand X Pictures, Dover Art, Photodisc, Shutterstock

Publications International, Ltd., has made every effort to locate the owners of all copyrighted material to obtain permission to use the selections that appear in this book. Any errors or omissions are unintentional; corrections, if necessary, will be made in future editions.

Scripture quotations are taken from the New Revised Standard Version of the Bible. Copyright © 1989 by the Division of Christian Education of the National Council of the Churches of Christ in the United States of America. Used by permission. All rights reserved.